my revision notes

AQA GCSE (9–1) History

MIGRATION, EMPIRES AND THE PEOPLE

c790 TO THE PRESENT DAY

Derek Moir

Thabo Stuck

HODDER
EDUCATION
AN HACHETTE UK COMPANY

The Publishers would like to thank the following for permission to reproduce copyright material.

Photo credits

p.11 © Visual Arts Resource / Alamy Stock Photo; **p.23** Public Domain via Wikimedia Commons (The engraving was copied by Paul Revere Design from a design by Henry Pelham); **p.33** © 1900 by Keppler & Schwarzmann via Library of Congress Prints and Photographs Division Washington, D.C. 20540 USA; **p.41** © Punch Cartoon Library / TopFoto; **p.45** © Fine Art Images/Heritage Images/Getty Images

Acknowledgements

Every effort has been made to trace all copyright holders, but if any have been inadvertently overlooked, the Publishers will be pleased to make the necessary arrangements at the first opportunity.

Although every effort has been made to ensure that website addresses are correct at time of going to press, Hodder Education cannot be held responsible for the content of any website mentioned in this book. It is sometimes possible to find a relocated web page by typing in the address of the home page for a website in the URL window of your browser.

Hachette UK's policy is to use papers that are natural, renewable and recyclable products and made from wood grown in well-managed forests and other controlled sources. The logging and manufacturing processes are expected to conform to the environmental regulations of the country of origin.

Orders: please contact Hachette UK Distribution, Hely Hutchinson Centre, Milton Road, Didcot, Oxfordshire, OX11 7HH. Telephone: +44 (0)1235 827827. Email: education@hachette.co.uk Lines are open from 9 a.m. to 5 p.m., Monday to Friday. You can also order through our website: www.hoddereducation.co.uk

ISBN: 9781398312357

First published in 2021 by

Hodder Education,
An Hachette UK Company
Carmelite House
50 Victoria Embankment
London EC4Y 0DZ

www.hoddereducation.co.uk

Impression number 10 9 8 7 6 5 4 3 2

Year   2025 2024 2023

Cover photo © alexanderbaumann - stock.adobe.com
Illustrations by Integra Software Services Ltd.
Typeset in India by Integra Software Services Ltd.
Printed in the UK by Ashford Colour Press

A catalogue record for this title is available from the British Library.

My revision planner

CONTENT TASKS

British Thematic Study

How the Thematic Study will be examined

Overview of the Thematic Study

It covers a long time-span (about 1,000 years). It is about the history of Britain, not the wider world.

In this book we cover the Thematic Study:

■ Britain: Migration, empires and the people: c790 to the present day.

Thematic studies focus on change and continuity over a long period of time:

■ The study examines key developments which affected Britain – including social, political and economic developments.

■ You will consider the significance of those different developments for people's health or for who holds power.

■ You will identify similarities and differences between periods.

■ You will assess the amount of change and continuity across periods.

■ You will consider the role of factors in causing or preventing change. Factors include: war, religion, government, economic resources, science and technology, ideas such as imperialism, Social Darwinism and civilisation, and the role of individuals.

■ You will also use lots of sources and you will evaluate them for usefulness.

There are various key skills you will need for the Thematic Study

Comprehending and evaluating sources – you will need to be able to look carefully at the content and provenance of a source and use your own knowledge in order to judge its usefulness for understanding a topic

Comparing events – you will need to identify key features of events or developments, from different time periods, and explain how similar or different they are

THE THEMATIC STUDY

Explaining developments – you will need to identify and explain the impact of a development both at the time and over time

Comparing factors – you will need to use evidence to compare the role of several different factors across time

Coming to overall judgements – you will need to make sophisticated judgements based upon the range of evidence used in your answer. You will need to write these in a clear and persuasive manner

There are four main question types in the Thematic Study

This will be Section A of your Paper 2. It is worth 44 marks in total. You will be asked the following types of question.

1 **How useful is this source?**   (8 marks)

You will be given a source and have to study both its content and provenance. You will have to use your own contextual knowledge to explain how useful the source is for understanding the period or topic.

2 **Explain the significance of ...**   (8 marks)

You will be given a key event, person, group or development. You will need to identify and explain the importance of this both at the time and in a later period.

3 **Compare/in what ways are they similar or different?**   (8 marks)

You will be given two events, developments or individuals/groups – usually from different periods. You will need to identify the features of each and identify ways in which they are similar or different.

4 **Essay question on the role of factors**   (16 marks + 4 SPaG)

You will be pointed to one factor which caused or prevented change and will have to judge the importance of this factor in comparison to other factors you have studied. These factors could include war, religion, government, economic resources, science and technology, ideas such as imperialism, Social Darwinism and civilisation or the role of individuals. You will need to evaluate at least two factors and come to a judgement on which was more important.

How we help you develop your exam skills

- The **Revision tasks** help you build understanding and skills step by step. For example:

Role of factors helps you to identify the impact of the key factors.

Activities focused on **comparing periods or events** will help to structure your thinking about similarities and differences over time.

Flow chart activities will help you to understand the narrative of events and consider the links between them.

Improve the paragraph style activities will help you to develop your understanding of how to present your ideas for the exam.

Develop detail/explanation style activities will help you to improve your ability to explain impacts.

- The **practice questions** give you exam style questions.
- **Exam focus** on pages 45–47 gives you model answers for each question type.

Plus:

There are **annotated model answers** for every practice question online at www.hoddereducation.co.uk/myrevisionnotesdownloads.

1.1 The Viking invasions

> **Key point**
>
> This Viking period of interacting with Britain started with piracy and plunder and ended with a North Sea empire ruled by a Dane – King Cnut.

> **TIP**
>
> These seven factors are a central part of this course as they affect change and continuity. These will be referred to throughout the book and are often interrelated – look for links between these through different time periods. See page 44 for an explanation of these factors. At the end of each chapter you will be asked to create your own table on these factors.

There were many factors which impacted on migration and Britain's dealings with the world 790–1560

- **Religion:** Vikings were heathens. Anglo-Saxons were Christian. Vikings made no attempt to convert Anglo-Saxons. **Christianity** was a unifying force for Anglo-Saxons. Normans made major reforms to the English Church – they replaced English bishops with Norman bishops and introduced the revolutionary gothic style of architecture for cathedrals.

- **Government:** Vikings ruled through the Danelaw. Alfred the Great created a new law code, written in Old English. The Normans created the Domesday Book to record the country's wealth. They then used this to tax the population. New legal codes were written in Latin.

- **Ideas:** Europe had converted to Christianity during the early Middle Ages. From the tenth century, the popes were attempting to maintain the unity of **Christendom**. The feudal system subjugated Anglo-Saxons to Norman barons. Normans also introduce the chivalric code.

- **Science and technology:** Viking longships were cutting-edge technology and were used to explore new lands and to transport economic goods, treasure and enslaved people internationally.

- **War:** Viking longships were the height of modern weapons technology. The Normans introduced knights and over 500 castles.

- **Economic resources:** Vikings were excellent traders and enslavement was at the heart of this. Dublin was a major slave trade town. Doomsday Book was collated by the Normans to assess wealth and tax the people.

- **Individuals:** Alfred the Great led the Saxon resistance to the Vikings and defeated the Danish leader Guthrum, which resulted in many Vikings converting to Christianity. William the Conqueror successfully invaded England and controlled it by establishing a ruthless military and political regime.

Vikings and Anglo-Saxons were very different

- During the Viking period, England was a divided land – the **heptarchy** – seven different kingdoms, which were often at war with each other. However, the kingdoms were united in that most people had Anglo-Saxon heritage and were Christian.

- Vikings were very different from the English. They were from Norway and Denmark and were heathens – non-Christians. They seemed to fear no one, looked very fierce and regarded death in war as glorious.

- As Vikings began to invade England from 792, many of the English believed the Vikings had been sent as a punishment from God.

Vikings invaded England to plunder and conquer

- The Vikings invaded England to gain wealth.
  - They soon found that monasteries and churches contained many riches as many religious objects were made from gold. Rich and powerful English people would leave large donations of gold and precious objects at monasteries and in return the monks would pray for their souls.
  - Monks could be sold as enslaved people – they were easy to capture as they did not fight back and were easily transportable in longships.

- England was an easy target because it was politically divided. If one area was well defended, the Vikings just attacked another looking for gold and enslaved people. Monasteries were easy to attack because they were undefended.

- The first Viking attack was in 793 at Lindisfarne in Northumbria at the monastery which was a shrine to St Cuthbert. Vikings then began to spread terror along the coast and inland as they invaded looking for more riches to plunder.

- After 865, the reason for Viking invasions changed – they wanted to conquer and colonise England to expand their trading routes, gain the prestige of an empire, and settle and farm in the fertile country.

- Vikings can be defined as an unregulated merchant warrior class.

The Danelaw kingdom was created as a result of the Viking conquest

- The **Anglo-Saxon Chronicle** details the landing of a Great Heathen Army in East Anglia and Northumbria in 865. This army was far greater than previous Viking invasions as they wanted to conquer and colonise an area of land.

- York (Jorvik) was used by the Vikings as a base from which to attack the Anglo-Saxon kings that surrounded them. It became the centre of Viking **commerce** and later the capital of the Danelaw kingdom.

- The Anglo-Saxon armies of Wessex and Mercia combined to defeat the Viking advance at Nottingham. To stop any further attacks the Mercians agreed to pay the Vikings to leave – the **Danegeld**. However, Vikings ignored this agreement and conquered Mercia in 874.

- Vikings from Norway and Denmark settled in the area they had conquered. This area was called **Danelaw** as it had mostly Danish migrants and was ruled by Danish law.

- Anglo-Saxons who lived in the Danelaw were not forced to change their religion and remained Christian.

- After a while Danes and Anglo-Saxons lived peacefully in Danelaw. There was intermarriage and a merging of Anglo-Dane cultures, laws, food and language. Common English words such as Wednesday, Thursday, skin and sky are Norse.

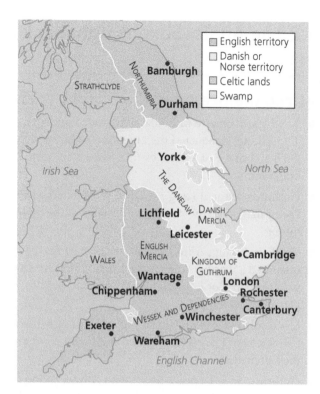

A map showing the Danelaw after the treaty of Alfred and Guthrum in 879

 Test yourself

1 What was the Danelaw?
2 Where was the first Viking attack on a monastery?
3 Explain the term Danegeld.

> **TIP**
>
> Stop! Think! Plan!
>
> There are 15 minutes of thinking and planning time built into the exam time – make sure you use them.

 Practice question

Explain the significance of the Viking invasion on Britain.   (8 marks)

 Role of factors

Question 4 of your exam will ask you to explain the role of factors in causing an event. Write some sentences to explain how the following were factors in the Viking invasions. One is completed for you as an example.

Factor	Explanation
Science and technology	
War	
Religion	
Economic resources	

1.2 The Anglo-Saxons fight back against Viking rule

Alfred the Great led the English resistance

- The Danish empire in England expanded under Guthrum, the Danish king. The Vikings conquered the kingdoms of Northumbria (867), East Anglia (869) and much of Mercia by 877. Wessex remained the only Anglo-Saxon kingdom.

- Guthrum defeated King Alfred of Wessex at the battle of Chippenham. The Danes massacred most of the inhabitants of the town and Alfred went into hiding.

- While in hiding, Alfred was able to contact his top commanders, who organised a massive counterattack against Guthrum's armies. The English won the battle of Edington in 878 and laid siege to Chippenham until the Danes surrendered.

- Upon surrender Guthrum and 29 of his commanders converted to Christianity. They were baptised at Alfred's court and accepted Alfred as their godfather.

- Guthrum signed a peace treaty with Alfred, fixing the borders of the Danelaw territory with himself as king of East Anglia and Alfred as king of the rest of England.

- Alfred realised that the peace treaty was not enough to prevent further Viking invasions so he reorganised the army and built strong defensive fortresses – burhs – permanently guarded by well-trained soldiers. He also ordered the creation of an English navy.

Alfred began the process of uniting England into one country

- Alfred managed to unite the Anglo-Saxons to fight for him by promoting himself as the defender of Christianity against heathens.

- After decades of anarchy in England, Alfred's armies eventually managed to defeat the Vikings and even win back some territory from Danish control.

- Alfred wanted England to be a united country and his victories made this seem possible.

- Alfred is remembered as a wise ruler who introduced a new law code and schools to train priests and secular administrators (judges, etc.), and encouraged the nobles at court to study as well as fight.

- According to a commissioned biography by Bishop Asser, Alfred was a brave, resourceful and religious man who was generous to the Church and wanted to rule fairly.

- After Alfred's death, his son Edward became king and continued to fight the Danes in England.

Key point

As the Vikings did not impose any change of religion on English Christians this enabled Alfred the Great to use Christianity to help develop a unified English identity. This led to the English fighting back against Viking control.

Alfred the Great, 849–899

- Alfred became king of Wessex after his brother Ethelred died in 871.
- He fought many battles with the Danes, eventually beating them in 878. The peace treaty split England between Alfred and Guthrum.
- Alfred and his wife Ealhswith had five children. Their son Edward became king after Alfred's death.

Guthrum, d. 890

- Guthrum was a skilled Viking warrior who was a leader of the Great Heathen Army that conquered much of eastern England.
- He lost to Alfred at the Battle of Edington in 878 and converted to Christianity in exchange for continuing as king of East Anglia.
- He became allies with Alfred and defended Alfred's interests in East Anglia against any future attacks.

England was ruled as one country by the mid-tenth century

- Edward's son Athelstan became the first king to control the whole of England, around 927. He defeated the Danes in the final large battle at Brunanburh in 937.
- Eric Bloodaxe remained the Danish king of Northumbria until he died in 954, after which all Danish warriors left England. Many second- or third-generation migrants remained to farm and trade.
- There were no further Viking raids for 25 years; however, by 980, they had returned. By 991, the English king Aethelred (The Unready) was paying vast sums in Danegeld to prevent Viking attacks.
- By this time the Danes had conquered part of northern France (that became Normandy) and were able to rest, restock and rearm there and prepare for the next raid a short distance away over the English Channel.
- Aethelred and his advisers secured a strategic marriage with the sister of Duke Richard II of Normandy. Emma of Normandy (see page 10) became the Queen of England in spring 1002.

(see page 10)

 Test yourself

1 Give three examples of how Alfred ruled as king.
2 Why did Aethelred, king of England, marry Emma of Normandy?
3 Why did many Vikings stay when their warriors left?

 Key individuals

Creating contact cards for the key individuals is a great way of organising your thoughts on how historical factors have affected individuals and how key individuals have affected historical factors.

Use this as your template to complete contact cards when asked to do so throughout the book.

	Key individual: Alfred the Great
War	
Religion	
Government	
Economic resources	
Science and technology	
Ideas	

 Key events

Complete the flow chart to summarise how England became one country.

First Viking raid 792				927 England is united
Vikings attack Lindisfarne in Northumbria				Athelstan is the first king to control the whole of England

Practice question

Explain the significance of Alfred the Great to Anglo-Saxon England.

(8 marks)

TIP

Anglo-Saxon names are very confusing and difficult to spell so make sure that you practise. Make flashcards – this can be done using Quizlet.

1.3 King Cnut, Emma of Normandy and the North Sea Empire

> **Key point**
>
> The intermarriage of King Cnut and Emma of Normandy helped to consolidate and strengthen his power base.

The St Brice's Day Massacre led to Viking revenge and Cnut of Denmark became king of England

- By 1002, Aethelred was still plagued by Viking raids. He decided to act and ordered a massacre of all Danes living in English territory. Historians are unclear about exactly what Aethelred meant by this as there were large numbers of Danes and people of Viking descent who had settled in England by then so it would have been impossible to kill them all. However, it is clear that many Danes were murdered on 13 November 1002 following Aethelred's order. It was St Brice's Day.

- Aethelred's nickname 'The Unready' really means 'ill advised' in Old English.

- Those murdered in the St Brice's Day Massacre probably included the sister of Danish king Sweyn Forkbeard (Gunhilde). Her husband, Pallig Tokesen, a Dane who had been made the Earl of Devon by Aethelred, was probably also murdered.

- In revenge, Sweyn led Viking attacks on England. By 1013 Aethelred and his sons had fled the country and Sweyn became king of England.

- Sweyn ruled England for only a few weeks before he died. His son Cnut succeeded him but faced a few years of fighting against Aethelred, who had returned to England, before he could declare himself king of England in 1016 after Aethelred's death.

Cnut the Great and Emma of Normandy ruled England, which became part of the North Sea Empire, for 19 years

- The English, led by Edmund Ironside, and the Danes, led by Cnut, fought many battles and the land ended up being split between the two leaders. After a three-year fight for kingship, Cnut ruled England for 19 years. It was generally a time of peace and prosperity.

- Cnut's law code was issued in 1020 – as a result, Viking pillaging stopped and Danish warriors were sent back to Denmark by 1020.

- To cement his rule, Cnut married Emma of Normandy, the widow of King Aethelred. This helped to legitimise his rule as she was the Queen of England.

- Cnut organised the country well and established earldoms which he asked reliable Anglo-Saxons to control. One of these earls, Godwin, was the father of the future King Harold II.

- Cnut was also very careful to treat Church leaders well and had good relations with the Pope in Rome. He visited Rome in 1027 and negotiated reduced payments for English travellers to Rome and created new English archbishops. Cnut rebuilt and repaired all churches that had been damaged by the Vikings.

- Cnut believed in the Danelaw, the authority of the Church and the divine right to rule.

- He arranged for his daughter to marry the Holy Roman Emperor's (Conrad II) son and for his sister to marry the Duke of Normandy. This opened up relations and created alliances, which were useful for his rule in the future.

- Cnut succeeded his brother as King of Denmark in 1018, then he conquered Norway in 1028. His

Cnut the Great, 995–1035 ✔	Emma of Normandy, c.985–1052 ✗
• As a son of Sweyn Forkbeard, King of Denmark, Cnut was chosen as King of England after Sweyn's death. • He was Christian, like most Danes of the time. • He became king of the North Sea Empire in 1028 after conquering Norway. • His rule was peaceful and prosperous.	• Emma was the sister of Duke Richard II of Normandy. They were great-great-grandchildren of Rollo, the Viking who became the first ruler of Normandy in the early tenth century. • Emma was a devout Christian and was strongly committed to helping the Church. • In 1002 she married King Aethelred of England. They had three children, including Edward, who ruled as King of England from 1042 to 1066. • In 1017 she married King Cnut of England. They had two children, including Harthacnut, who ruled as King of England from 1040 to 1042. • Emma therefore was crowned Queen of England twice and was mother to two more English kings.

empire of England, Denmark and Norway is known as the North Sea Empire, which Cnut ruled peacefully for nearly 20 years. This greatly increased political and economic trade between Scandinavia, Britain and Europe, resulting in greater prosperity.

Emma of Normandy played a leading role in England as queen and mother

- Emma of Normandy was Queen of England when married to Aethelred. She was then Queen of England again and also Queen of Denmark and Norway when she was married to Cnut. She was the mother of two kings of England – Harthacnut (1040–42), then Edward (1042–66).
- For 50 years Emma was an influential figure in English society and politics. She had her own land centred around Winchester, which was the royal seat of Wessex with a cathedral and Saxon royal treasury.
- During the reign of Cnut she played a more active role in ruling England alongside her husband and he often took her advice.
- She was strongly committed to the Church and had connections with leading priests such as Stigand, who became Archbishop of Canterbury under her son Edward.
- When Cnut died in 1035, his son Harold Harefoot (from his first wife) became King of England. Harthacnut, his son with Emma, became King of Denmark and Emma worked hard to gain the throne of England for him as well.

 Practice question

Question 1 in your exam will ask you to assess the usefulness (utility) of a source for a given purpose. For example:

How useful is Source A to an historian studying the Viking invasions of England? Explain your answer using Source A and your contextual knowledge. (8 marks)

SOURCE A The Battle of Assandun, England, on 18 October 1016, manuscript illustration showing King Edmund II (died November 1016) in full armour charging Cnut the Great (c.995–1035). The English are on the left, the Danes are on the right

- When Harold Harefoot died in 1040, Harthacnut became King of England until his unexpected death in 1042. He was the last Dane to rule England.
- Emma's position and influence were so great that her son with Aethelred, Edward, succeeded his half-brother. He was King of England until 1066.

 Test yourself

1 Was the St Brice's Day Massacre a success or a failure? Explain why.
2 Give three examples of how Cnut ruled as king.

 Key individuals

Complete contact cards to show the significance of Cnut and Emma of Normandy (one for each).

	Cnut/Emma of Normandy
War	
Religion	
Government	
Economic resources	
Science and technology	
Ideas	

 Develop the detail

The diagram below gives reasons for Viking invasions of England. Add supporting detail.

TIP

Structure: **two** paragraphs.

For **utility** questions, you need to identify **two** important points made or shown in the source and explain why they are useful, with evidence. Structure your answer in two paragraphs, one discussing each point.

1.4 A Norman kingdom and 'Angevin Empire'

After the Norman Conquest of 1066 England became part of an Angevin Empire and was ruled by French families – the Normans, the Angevins and the Plantagenets

- Duke William of Normandy believed that King Edward of England had promised him the English throne. He also had a bloodline claim as Emma of Normandy's great-nephew. When Edward died in 1066, his brother-in-law, Harold Godwinson, became king. William decided to try to take the throne by force. He invaded England and defeated Harold at the Battle of Hastings.

- William therefore became King William I of England as well as Duke of Normandy and spent his time between his two realms.

- William dealt harshly with Anglo-Saxon uprisings and strengthened royal control by building more than 500 castles to maintain Norman interests. Laws were now written in Latin, not English.

- When William died, England and Normandy were divided between his sons, but his third son, Henry I, reunited the two in 1106. Henry I named his daughter Matilda as his successor, but when he died in 1135 she was challenged by her cousin, Stephen. Their dispute became known as 'the Anarchy' because of the lawlessness and civil war that engulfed England.

- Matilda was married to Geoffrey, Count of Anjou, a large region of France. He managed to seize control of Normandy while fighting continued in England. Stephen negotiated with Matilda and Geoffrey to remain King of England until he died, then their son, Henry of Anjou, would replace Stephen.

- The Counts of Anjou were known as the **Angevins**, so in 1154 Henry II became the first Angevin King of England as well as ruling Normandy, Anjou and Aquitaine in France.

- During this period, many French people migrated to England. As with the Vikings before them, their customs and aspects of language became integrated with those of the English and developed an Anglo-Norman identity.

Henry II expanded the Angevin Empire to become the largest dominion of any English king after the invasion of Ireland in 1171

- Asserting control throughout the Angevin Empire was difficult because it was so large. England was particularly hard because of the years of anarchy. However, Henry II managed to restore royal authority by increasing finances and reorganising the justice system.

- Ireland was a collection of small kingdoms with one high king ruling over them all. It was a Christian country, but unlike the Angevin Empire, it was independent of the Pope. In 1155, Pope Adrian IV (who was English) gave Henry II the authority of the Church to take over Ireland.

- Henry II invaded Ireland in 1171 and went on to conquer areas that had previously been controlled by a Welsh-Norman lord, Richard 'Strongbow' de Clare.

- Henry stayed in Ireland for six months building castles to ensure Angevin control, but Irish lords fought back. In 1175, Henry signed the Treaty of Windsor with the High King of Ireland, Rory O'Conner, who agreed to pay homage to the King of England. Henry became feudal overlord of about

> **Key point**
>
> England became part of a large empire which included part of France between 1066 and 1199 but much of the land in France was lost by King John.

three-quarters of Ireland. He directly owned and ruled the rest of it – known as 'The Pale'. In 1177, Henry named his youngest son John as Lord of Ireland.

The actions of King John reduced the size of the Angevin Empire as he lost large areas of land in France

- When Richard I, eldest surviving son of Henry II, went to fight in the Third Crusade, his younger brother John plotted with Philip II, King of France, to divide the Angevin Empire between them. This attempt failed when Richard returned.
- Philip II turned on John after he became king on Richard's death in 1199 and invaded Normandy, but John managed to drive him out.
- John's actions then led to further war with France. He refused to pay homage to Philip as his overlord and he married Isabelle of Angoulême, who had been promised to a powerful Frenchman who appealed to Philip for help. Philip then inflicted successive defeats on English armies until they were pushed out of Normandy in 1204.
- John was forced to sign the Great Charter (**Magna Carta**), which limited royal power, in 1215. English barons were tired of John's loss of France, his scheming and his high war taxes.
- John signed the charter only to buy time to raise forces to destroy the rebel barons. The rebels then invited Prince Louis of France to invade England in 1216 to help them. Louis' army invaded and forced John into retreat.
- After John's death in 1216, the English were led by William Marshal, acting as regent for John's nine-year-old son, Henry III. 1215–17 was a crucial time in the development of an English national identity – although the hated John was gone, the French were an occupying army and the English rallied against a common enemy.

 Test yourself

1 Explain how migration affected England during this period.
2 Give three examples of how Henry II expanded the Angevin Empire.
3 Explain why the empire reduced in size under King John.

 Key events

Complete the blank boxes to show your knowledge of important events during this period.

Battle of Hastings 1066					Death of King John 1216

 Key individuals

Create contact cards for King Henry II and King John

 Practice question

Explain the significance of Henry II's empire in the development of Anglo-Irish relations. (8 marks)

Henry II, 1133–89

- Henry was born and raised in France and became Count of Anjou and ruler of Normandy after the death of his father, Geoffrey, in c.1150.
- His marriage to Eleanor of Aquitaine in 1151 added the large French region of Aquitaine to his empire.
- He became King of England in 1154 and invaded Ireland in 1171 to try to establish Angevin authority there.
- An incredibly hard-working and energetic man, he split his time between all the lands he ruled, though he spent most time in France (approximately 21 years out of 35) as that was his largest territory.

King John, 1166/67–1216

- John was the youngest surviving son of Henry II and Eleanor of Aquitaine.
- He became king in 1199 when his elder brother, Richard I, died.
- John is regarded as a poor ruler. His reign is famous for the limits of royal power imposed through the Great Charter (the Magna Carta).
- John's actions led to frequent wars with France and the loss of Normandy to the French king Philip II.

TIP

You may find less information on some factors during their reign; however, these are still important. It is often the case that major reforms/developments had taken place in previous periods and there was less change and more continuity of previous policy/economic/religious and scientific developments.

1.5 The birth of English identity: The Hundred Years War and its impact on England's development

REVISED

The Hundred Years War was an attempt by English kings to regain land in France

- Henry III (1216–72) tried to regain the authority of the crown in England. His son Edward I (1272–1307) largely did this and attempted to control Wales (with some success) and conquer Scotland (with little success). However, his son Edward II (1307–1327) was a weak and deeply unpopular king. He gave up on his attempted conquest of Scotland and desperately wanted to keep hold of the only remaining lands in France – Aquitaine. To do this he sent his wife to pay homage to the French king.

- Edward III wanted to recapture the prestige that had been lost by his father by regaining land in France.

- When Philip VI of France confiscated Aquitaine in 1337 and expected Edward III to pay homage, Edward chose war. This was the start of a huge period of conflict between England and France, known as the Hundred Years War.

> **Key point**
>
> The Hundred Years War was a period of conflict between England and France that led to England finally losing all the Angevin Empire, except for Calais, but its victories of small English armies over large French ones did help give birth to an English identity.

During the period of war, England won key battles but failed to hold on to land in France

- The Battle of Crecy (1346):
  - Edward III sailed to Normandy with 15,000 men in 1346. The Battle at Crecy was a stunning victory for the English over Philip VI's larger army. Edward chose the perfect location and used longbows and cannon to beat the French.
  - As a result of the battle the French could not help Calais, which England won in 1347. Calais was ruled by England's king for the next 200 years.

- The Battle of Poitiers (1356):
  - Led by Edward III's son, Edward the Black Prince, the Battle of Poitiers was another spectacular victory for the English and a humiliating defeat for France as King John II and his son were both captured.
  - Although French knights had improved their armour to protect against longbows, the archers simply aimed at the horses and the English infantry massacred the knights as their armour was too heavy.

- The Battle of Agincourt (1415):
  - Edward III won land in France, but decades of political instability in England followed his death and France retook many English gains.
  - In 1413 Edward's great-grandson, Henry V, was crowned at the age of 29 and immediately planned to invade France with 6,000 men to reclaim his family's land. Henry was a great strategist and secured some quick victories, and in October 1415 he marched on Calais.
  - French forces outnumbered them by four to one when they met outside the village of Agincourt.
  - The French were confident of victory. But Henry was a skilled battlefield commander and kept his men at a distance from the French, which allowed his archers to devastate the French cavalry (who got stuck in the mud) with their longbows.

The Hundred Years War had an impact on 'Englishness' as it led to the birth of English identity and England's future development as Angevin lands were lost for ever

- The apex of English rule over France was the capture of Paris, which the English held from 1415 until Henry V's death in 1422. Henry forced the French king to accept him as his lawful heir.

- However, once Henry V had died, the English found it hard to hold on to France. They were defeated at the siege of Orleans in 1429 by Charles VII, whose army was led by Joan of Arc. Then Charles VII successfully united the French against the English, who were beaten in the final battle of the Hundred Years War in 1453 at the Battle of Castillon. This time the French had mastered new military technology – artillery – which they used to break the English charge.

- The Hundred Years War was pivotal in forging an English identity, however:

  ○ The victories of Edward III and especially Henry V's victory at Agincourt saw a small army of all social classes beat a much larger force. Many saw this as a miracle and large crowds gathered in London for the victory parade.

  ○ During the Hundred Years War, for the first time since the Norman Conquest, England was ruled by kings who spoke and wrote in English as their first language rather than French. English has been the language of government in England ever since.

  ○ To many in England, the seemingly impossible victories also made it appear that God was on their side. As such, it gave the English a sense of destiny and played a central role in shaping English identity in centuries to come.

 Test yourself

1 In your opinion, who won the Hundred Years War?
2 When was the Battle of Agincourt?
3 Why might the Hundred Years War be seen as a major factor in creating an English identity? Give three examples.

 Topic summary

Complete the table, giving reasons for the Hundred Years War in the left column and the key consequences of the Hundred Years War in the right column.

Reasons for the Hundred Years War	Consequences of the Hundred Years War

 Change and continuity tables

Complete the factors table and change & continuity table for Part 1 Conquered and conquerors. See page 44 for how to create this table.

 Practice question

Explain the significance of the Hundred Years War in Britain.   (8 marks)

> **TIP**
>
> When answering 'significance' questions you should consider **two** points in depth. For this question, for example, you could consider developments in warfare and in English identity. Write a paragraph on each.

Part 2 Looking west

2.1 Sugar and the Caribbean

REVISED

> **Key point**
>
> The sixteenth and seventeenth centuries marked an age of transatlantic exploration, religious change and economic development for England. The slave trade began early on in European colonisation of the Americas, including in England's first Caribbean colony, Barbados.

There were many changes in England in the sixteenth and seventeenth centuries which impacted on the factors that influenced Britain's dealings with the world

- **Religion:** After the Reformation countries began breaking away from the Catholic Church. England became a Protestant country in 1534 under Henry VIII. This led to persecution, which would spark migration from England to places such as America.

- **War:** Conflict with the Spanish in the sixteenth century involved many sea-based skirmishes but never out-and-out war. These clashes took place near to home but also as far away as the Caribbean. By the late eighteenth century England was at war with the Americans, who were fighting for independence.

- **Government:** From 1603 after King James VI of Scotland became King James I of England, England and Scotland were ruled by the same person. Both countries became united with the 1707 Act of Union.

- **Ideas:** The renaissance era saw developments in art and culture across Europe, with influences from around the world finding their way to English shores. These new ideas saw Europeans also seek to reach lands they had never been to before.

- **Science and technology:** Developments in navigation and faster, well-armed ships meant that Europeans were able to travel and migrate around the world more easily. In 1492 Christopher Columbus reached what is thought to be the Bahamas. Under Queen Elizabeth I, English seafarers also began exploring the world.

- **Economic resources:** The discovery of exotic goods such as tobacco and sugar sparked a rush of people migrating to the Caribbean and America to seek their fortunes.

- **Individuals:** Men such as Walter Raleigh and John Hawkins began opening England up to the world for personal profit, prestige and favour.

England's first involvement in the Caribbean was through piracy and plunder

- By the sixteenth century, Spain and Portugal had colonised much of the Americas and had a monopoly on trade there. Ships loaded with riches frequently voyaged back to Spain and Portugal. English sailors began taking advantage of this through piracy (attacking and robbing the ships).

- Queen Elizabeth I wanted to damage Spain and gain wealth for England so she licensed some of England's best sailors such as John Hawkins and Francis Drake to attack and rob Spanish ships. They were known as privateers. There was little difference between privateers and pirates – both stole and used violence.

- Overseas expansion during this period was privately funded and English navy ships were privately owned and equipped. New ships, galleons, were being built. These were much faster and better armed, underpinning England's future imperial expansion.

- The trade monopoly meant that anyone trading with the Spanish Caribbean colonies had to pay a tax to Spanish authorities. Smuggling therefore became profitable for many English merchants.

- English privateers, pirates, smugglers and merchants saw America for themselves and brought back to England tales and examples of the great wealth to be found there.

Sir John Hawkins was England's first major slave trader who pioneered the triangular trade

- In 1562 Hawkins led a successful raid on Portuguese ships off the coast of West Africa, capturing expensive goods and 300 enslaved African people. He then smuggled them into the Caribbean to the island of Santa Domingo (now the Dominican Republic), selling them for a huge sum.

- Hawkins is seen as a pioneer of the triangular trade between England, West Africa and the Caribbean as he inspired others to do the same thing. The slave trade would be dominated by the British until it was banned by Parliament in 1807 after an abolition movement that lasted nearly 50 years.

Barbados was the first English Caribbean colony, which became dominated by sugar plantations that used enslaved African labour

- Barbados was established as an English colony in 1627 by William Courten.

- Like America, the Caribbean islands offered opportunities to grow crops that could not be cultivated in England. The first Europeans to go to the Caribbean soon discovered that its climate was ideal for growing sugar cane. Many crops thrived there, so it was seen as a great opportunity for people to make their fortune.

- Many of the first to travel to Barbados were **indentured servants**, poor people who had travelled to the Americas trying to find opportunities to own some land and improve their lives. Some, mostly Quakers, went to Barbados because their religious views were causing them trouble in England.

- Sugar was little used in Europe because it was quite rare at the beginning of the seventeenth century. However, as Europeans acquired a taste for it, demand exploded and by 1667, 80 per cent of Barbados was planted with sugar cane.

- Growing sugar cane required expensive equipment, quite a large plot of land and lots of labour. This meant that sugar **plantations** developed. They were owned by wealthy English men and women who all used enslaved labour to farm them.

- The successes for England in sugar colonies like Barbados and other parts of the Caribbean spurred the English government to sanction the capture of Jamaica from Spain, which became a English colony in 1655.

1 Traders leave European ports headed for Africa with goods such as alcohol, tobacco and guns

3 In the Caribbean and the Americas, most enslaved people are sold to plantation owners to farm crops such as sugar, rice or tobacco. These are transported back to Europe

2 When they arrive in West Africa, they trade these goods with African people in exchange for prisoners from other tribes. Many enslaved people were also kidnapped. The enslaved people are loaded onto ships and sailed across the Atlantic

The trade triangle in three steps

Key individuals

Complete a contact card to show the significance of John Hawkins.

Sir John Hawkins, 1532–95

- John Hawkins was a sailor and pirate, who made vast amounts of money from capturing enslaved African people from the Portuguese in West Africa in 1562.
- Hawkins set up the West Africa Company and was the pioneer of the triangular trade.
- He helped to develop the English navy and was knighted in 1588 by Queen Elizabeth for leadership against the Spanish Armada.

Test yourself

1 Identify three reasons why England 'opened up' to the world by the early seventeenth century.

2 When did Christopher Columbus first explore America?

3 Who established the colony of Barbados and when?

4 What was the key **commodity** produced in Barbados?

Consider significance

Because significance can seem quite a vague idea it is easy to get sucked into including irrelevant details. All you really have to do with a significance question is explain one way the factor was significant at the time and one way it has been significant for people looking back from a later period.

Use your revision card on John Hawkins to complete a table on how Hawkins was significant at the time and in later periods.

TIP

When assessing usefulness, consider the motive of the person who created it.

Practice question

Explain the significance of John Hawkins to the development of the British Empire. (8 marks)

2.2 The development and impact of the slave trade

The development of the British slave trade

- Before 1700, the British slave trade remained quite small, mostly supplying enslaved African people to Spanish colonies. This started to develop because of increased demand in British colonies as well and the growing number of plantations in the Caribbean (then known as the West Indies) and British America.
- Britain came to dominate the transatlantic slave trade and in 1672 the Royal African Company was granted a monopoly over supplying enslaved people from West Africa to the Caribbean and the Americas.
- Between 1672 and 1689 the Royal African Company captured and trafficked 100,000 enslaved African people across the Atlantic.
- After the Royal African Company lost its monopoly, the number of independent slave traders increased.
- Demand for products 'foreign' to Europe, such as sugar from the Caribbean, tobacco from Virginia in the US and rice from South Carolina, significantly drove the slave trade. In 1700, 23,000 tons of sugar was unloaded at British docks; by 1800 that figure had grown to 245,000 tons.
- Overall, the British trafficked nearly 3 million enslaved African people. One out of six died due to the dreadful conditions on the ships.

> **Key point**
>
> The transatlantic slave trade greatly benefited the British economy. Until slavery was abolished in the nineteenth century, Britain trafficked nearly 3 million enslaved African people to America and the Caribbean.

The economic impact of the slave trade in Britain was huge

- The British companies and individuals who took part in the slave trade became wealthy. Some of the profits also benefited the British economy.
- Most plantation and slave owners stayed in Britain and visited their plantations only occasionally. These people became wealthy due to the low cost, high yield of slave labour. Many used their wealth to buy influence in Parliament as well as to build great buildings, buy luxury goods and commission works of art. Some used their wealth to do philanthropic work in Britain, which is ironic given the brutal origin of much of their wealth.
- The slave trade boosted other types of trade and businesses. This created thousands of jobs as the raw materials produced by enslaved African people were manufactured in Britain into goods, some of which generated huge profits when they were sold.
- The economy of British cities like Liverpool and Bristol particularly benefited from the transatlantic slave trade. Much of modern Britain's wealth accumulated through slavery.

The social impact of the slave trade on Britain was substantial

- The raw materials and new products brought by the slave trade had a big impact socially in Britain. For example, this changed the clothes people wore and the food and drink they consumed.
- The slave trade and slavery led to the belief that African people were inferior to Europeans. Racism and racial injustice continued long after the abolition of slavery and still exists today.
- Slavery caused divisions in British society at the time. Some felt that slavery was wrong, due to moral and religious beliefs. The Abolition Movement set out to change British law and make slavery illegal.

- Many owners of plantations and enslaved people in Parliament argued strongly for keeping the slave trade going, with some even arguing that capturing and trafficking African people from their homeland actually benefited those who were enslaved.

- The slave trade was finally abolished by Parliament in 1807 and in 1833 slave ownership was banned altogether. This occurred after a number of revolts by enslaved people in the Caribbean.

- Slave owners were paid substantial compensation when slavery was abolished, but no reparations were paid to those who had been enslaved. Plantations remained and many black people carried on working for the same masters as before.

- Ongoing injustices towards black people in the Caribbean would lead to uprisings such as the Morant Bay Rebellion in Jamaica in 1865.

- Britain's relationship with the Caribbean would continue to be a key part of the empire (see page 40).

- Large parts of West Africa were left economically and socially damaged by the enslavement of its people.

- Population growth slowed to such an extent it has been estimated that by 1850, Africa's population growth was halved.

 Test yourself

1 Which country had the monopoly on the slave trade in the seventeenth century?

2 How many enslaved people did the British transport?

3 What were the main crops grown on plantations that used slave labour?

 Consider significance

Question 2 will ask you about the significance of an event you have studied. For example:

Explain the significance of the transatlantic slave trade in the development of Britain. (8 marks)

Because significance can seem quite a vague idea it is easy to get sucked into including irrelevant details. All you really have to do with a significance question is explain one way the event was significant at the time and one way it has been significant for people looking back from a later period.

Copy and complete this grid to help you plan your answer to the exam-style question above.

Event or development	At the time (short term)	In later periods (long term)
The transatlantic slave trade		

 Role of factors

Record examples of each of the following factors affecting the development of the transatlantic slave trade:

- Economic resources
- Religion
- Government
- Ideas

TIP

When addressing significance, make sure you consider both short- and longer-term impacts.

2.3 Colonisation in North America

Virginia was the first British colony in America, established by Walter Raleigh in 1587

- Walter Raleigh was a sailor and privateer who voyaged to the Americas in the 1570s. He returned to England full of tales of his exciting adventures and soon became a favourite of Queen Elizabeth I.
- In 1584 he sent a group of English colonists to Roanoke Island. They failed, as did another group in 1587.
- In 1585 Raleigh received royal permission to establish an English colony on the east coast of North America. He called it Virginia, named after the queen.

The causes of British colonisation of America in the seventeenth century were mostly economic and religious

- Many people chose to migrate to America because of economic problems in Britain and economic opportunities in America:
  - Unemployment in England was quite high.
  - Most land in England was held by relatively few people and land was extremely expensive to buy.
  - Failed harvests meant many people were struggling for survival.
  - In contrast, America's vast areas of land were an attractive prospect – many wanted to grow crops and send these back to England for profit.
  - Buying passage to America and the right to settle there cost less than buying land in England.
- For some migrants a major factor in their decision to leave was their religious beliefs. Around 80,000 **Puritans** migrated to America between 1630 and 1641, just before the outbreak of the English Civil War in 1642:
  - Christian groups such as Puritans, Quakers and Catholics had suffered religious persecution in England since the Reformation in 1530. They wanted to escape this.
  - The chance of settling in a land where they could live according to their beliefs without interference from the Church of England or other religious beliefs was attractive to many.
- The two earliest settlements in British colonies were Jamestown and Plymouth. Jamestown attracted mostly economic migrants whereas Plymouth attracted mostly religious migrants.

> **Key point**
>
> America became the focal point of European colonisation in the Age of Discovery. Many people chose to migrate to North America in the sixteenth and seventeenth centuries for economic and religious reasons.

> **Sir Walter Raleigh, 1554–1618**
>
> - Raleigh was a famous sailor, soldier and privateer who became a favourite of Queen Elizabeth I.
> - Raleigh was given royal permission to set up the colony of Virginia.
> - He heard about great riches in South America and went to the area known as Guiana in 1595.

Colony	Motives	Aims	Consequences
Virginia	In 1606, King James I gave permission for businessmen to sail to Virginia in search of gold and land to grow crops.	The aim was to set up a settlement called Jamestown, which they did in 1607.	Facing initial hardships and hostilities with Indigenous Americans, many began growing tobacco, which was profitable. More Brits would arrive seeking fortunes.
Massachusetts (the Pilgrim Fathers)	Puritans, wanting to escape the persecution they faced because of their religious beliefs, left for America on the *Mayflower* in 1620.	The aim was to set up a colony, New Plymouth, where they could follow their religion without interference and establish trade with other colonies.	Setting up democratic principles and religious rules, the Pilgrim Fathers attracted nearly 20,000 colonists to Massachusetts by 1640.

- As people began to colonise British America, they soon realised that they needed workers to help them farm the vast areas of land. This led to many indentured servants migrating to America. Their travel was paid for and when they arrived they received food and housing in exchange for their labour for a set period of usually 4–7 years. Once this time was up, indentured servants were free to buy and work their own land.

- As time went on, indentured servants were replaced by forced migrants from Africa – enslaved people – because it was more profitable.

The settlement of the British colonies in America had a devastating impact on Indigenous Americans

- The colonies of Jamestown, New Plymouth and Massachusetts initially had positive relations with Indigenous American tribes. There were even some intermarriages.

- Over time, relations turned sour due to British mistreatment of Indigenous Americans. Raids and massacres were carried out by both sides as British colonists started to take more land.

- European diseases such as smallpox and measles, British expansion and conflict meant that many Indigenous American tribes were displaced and had to find new land, or were forced to adapt to European customs.

- In 1500 there were approximately 560,000 Indigenous Americans in British territories. By 1700 there were fewer than 280,000.

- Britain gained much of this land. There were 13 British colonies on the east coast where British immigrants could now thrive, at the expense of the Indigenous Americans.

 Test yourself

1 List three reasons why people chose to migrate to America.
2 What crop enabled people in Virginia to earn money?
3 How many people had migrated to Massachusetts by 1640?
4 List three impacts that the British colonies had on Indigenous Americans.

 Key individuals

Complete a contact card for Walter Raleigh (see page 20).

 Role of factors

Record examples of each of the following factors affecting colonisation in North Ameriica:
- War
- Religion
- Government
- Ideas
- Individuals
- Economics

 Practice question

Explain the significance of British migration to America in the development of the British Empire. (8 marks)

TIP

You must consider how migration to America impacted on Britain in the long term. Did this migration develop Britain in an economic sense? Did it trigger more migration in the long term?

2.4 The American War of Independence

The American War of Independence was a dispute between the Americans and the British that started over taxes

- The 13 British American colonies had a lot of autonomy – the people of these colonies made most of the decisions on how their colony was run through local assemblies.
- The Seven Years War of 1756–63 was was fought in defence of British colonies, including North America. It was extremely expensive, and many MPs in Britain thought that the American colonists should pay tax to Britain for debts incurred.
- The Stamp Act of 1765 was the first attempt by the British government to directly tax the American colonies.
- Many colonists resisted the tax because they did not have any representation in the British Parliament. They demanded: 'No taxation without representation.'
- This act was repealed within a year, only to be replaced by new taxes imposed in 1767.
- These new taxes led to protests that saw five colonists shot in the Boston Massacre of 1770.
- The colonists were particularly upset with taxes placed on tea. In 1773 some protestors boarded British ships in Boston and dumped 342 crates of tea into the harbour (known as the Boston Tea Party).
- Many felt that these acts had impeded their liberties.

The American War of Independence led to the loss of Britain's American colonies

- In July 1776 the 13 American colonies declared their independence from Britain.
- The British fought many battles against rebel American colonists. Not all colonists supported the rebels, however, and some in Britain were sympathetic to the rebel colonists.
- Eventually the British surrendered at Yorktown in 1781. The war officially ended in 1783 when the Treaty of Paris was signed.
- This was a massive blow to the prestige of Britain and its military prowess.
- Much of the American forces had been mainly comprised of local militia, who used guerrilla tactics to defeat the better equipped and trained British forces.
- The Americans were incredibly determined and had excellent military leaders such as George Washington. They were also supported by the French navy, which added to British difficulties with supplies and communications.
- Despite the war, America eventually became an important ally to Britain. Even today, America and Britain share what is called the 'Special Relationship'.
- By 1785 trade with America was back to the same rates as before the war.
- Britain started to look for opportunities to replace America as a colony. British interest in India therefore became more prominent.

Key point

England's 'opening up' to the Americas would lead to many people migrating and setting up new colonies, seeking opportunity and religious freedoms. The development of ideas about liberty would eventually lead to these colonies declaring themselves independent from England.

 Test yourself

1 Why did the colonists of British America become unhappy with the British?

2 When did the 13 colonies of British America declare independence?

3 What was the name of the treaty that ended the War of Independence?

Topic summary

Complete the table, giving reasons for the American War of Independence in the left column and the key consequences of the American War of Independence in the right column.

Reasons for the American War of Independence	Consequences of the American War of Independence

 Consider usefulness

How useful is Source A to an historian studying British colonisation in North America? Explain your answer using Source A and your contextual knowledge. (8 marks)

SOURCE A: An American poster published on 28 March 1770 showing the Boston Massacre of 5 March 1770 when British soldiers fired on a crowd of civilians. The title of the picture was, 'The Fruits of Arbitrary Power', or 'The Bloody Massacre'. The poster was reprinted many times. The massacre took place in front of the Royal Custom House and the Butchers Hall.

Make notes in a grid like this to plan an answer.

Provenance	Content
Who made it and why?	What does it say about attitudes of the British in America?
	From your knowledge of events, is this accurate?
How does this affect its usefulness?	How does this affect its usefulness?

 Practice question

Explain the significance of the American War of Independence to the British Empire. (8 marks)

TIP

A good way to show your understanding of significance is to focus on factors. For example, think about how the American War of Independence impacted the British Empire in terms of economic resources.

2.5 Migrants to and from Britain – three case studies

Religious persecution in France led to protestants (Huguenots) migrating to England

- France experienced a series of civil wars between 1560 and 1590 during which the ruling French Catholics persecuted the minority groups of Protestants, known as **Huguenots**.
- Hostilities reached their peak in 1572 when tens of thousands of Protestants were killed in the St Bartholomew's Day Massacre. To escape the persecution, many decided to flee to Protestant Britain.
- In 1598 the Edict of Nantes established religious freedom in France for Protestants, so Huguenot migration drastically decreased. However, in 1685 King Louis XIV revoked the Edict of Nantes. As a result, thousands once again left for England.

The Huguenots brought skills, contacts and wealth with them and they had a significant impact on Britain

- Between 40,000 and 50,000 Huguenots settled in England, often in big cities like London.
- Huguenots had often lived in urban areas so had skills in textile weaving and watch-making and worked in professions such as banking and the law. They therefore brought useful skills to England.
- Many Huguenots had been successful in business, bringing great wealth and well-established contacts with merchants oversees, especially in Holland, another Protestant country. This benefited England. For example, the Huguenots helped to set up the Bank of England in 1694.
- Many Huguenots successfully assimilated, learning the English language and worshipping in a Protestant manner.
- There was also anti-Huguenot feeling in England. Some felt they were stealing jobs or brought disease with them.

The Ulster Plantations was a plan to colonise part of Ireland with British Protestants

- England was confirmed as a Protestant nation during the reign of Queen Elizabeth I but Ireland remained Catholic, which frightened Elizabeth, who feared the Spanish might use Ireland as a base for invasion.
- The northern area of Ulster had a strong, proudly Catholic, independence group. This area was seen as ideal for a settlement of loyal Protestants to keep control of Ireland.
- In 1607 under the rule of James I, a plan was devised to colonise Ulster with Protestants loyal to him and to remove all Irish Catholics.

The Ulster Plantations had a huge impact on Britain and Ireland which is still felt today

- Many English and Scottish Protestants moved to Ulster to replace the Irish Catholic nobles who had fled the country. Others were moved from their land to make way for the Protestants, which created much resentment.

> **Key point**
> Religious turbulence in Europe and economic changes caused migration to, from and within Britain in the seventeenth and eighteenth centuries.

- However, the plan was to create a totally Protestant settlement, which was not achieved because the Protestant colonists needed workers so employed many Irish Catholics. By 1622 there were roughly 1,000 Protestant colonists compared with 4,000 Irish Catholics.

- The Ulster Plantations effectively created a divided community – of mainly wealthier Protestants and mainly poorer Catholics. The consequences would be enormous. While the rest of Ireland became an independent nation in the early twentieth century, Northern Ireland remained joined to Britain and the United Kingdom because by then the majority of the population was Protestant, with a very large Catholic minority.

The Highland Clearances led to mass migration from Britain

- In the early 1700s over half the people in Scotland lived in the Highlands, many in clans. Most Highlanders had strong loyalty to traditional Gaelic culture, speaking Gaelic, which was very similar to Irish.

- Most land in the Highlands were owned by a few wealthy landowners. The majority of Highlanders were tenant farmers who rented smallholdings called crofts from these landowners.

- From the late seventeenth century, but mostly from 1750 to 1800, some wealthy landowners decided to modernise the agricultural economy by turning their land over to sheep farming. This meant wide-scale eviction of the crofters from their land to make way for sheep farms.

- These forced evictions were widespread: 2,000 evictions in a day was not uncommon. Many were forced to seek work near the barren coastal land. Those who could not find workable land starved. Some who refused to move or were too old to do so were even killed.

- The Clearances became a motivation for mass Scottish emigration. Thousands emigrated abroad, the majority to British colonies such as Canada and New Zealand.

- As a result, the Scottish Highlands became sparsely populated, which continues to this day.

Test yourself

1 Why did the Huguenots flee France?

2 Why was Queen Elizabeth I concerned about Ireland?

3 Where did people migrate to after the Highland Clearances?

TIP

In 'explain two ways' questions, make sure you cover **two** ways in which the events were similar or different. If you only cover one way you lose half the marks straight away, but do not waste time trying to cover more than two ways as you won't get credit.

Practice question

Explain two ways in which the impact of the Huguenots on Britain was similar to that of the Pilgrim Fathers on America.   (8 marks)

Compare events

Question 3 will ask you to compare two key events from any part of the course. You will be asked to 'explain two ways' in which these events were either similar or different.

Make a list of similarities and differences between the Ulster Plantations and the Highland Clearances:

- Causes
- Events
- Consequences

Change and continuity tables

Complete the factors table and change and continuity table for Part 2 Looking West. See page 44.

3.1 Expansion in India

> **Key point**
>
> After the loss of the American colonies, British interests in India grew. India had valuable economic resources and was ruled by many difference princes who did not always get along. India was also a place where European powers jostled for control to increase their power in the world.

In the late eighteenth and the nineteenth centuries Britain came to dominate the world through different factors

- **War:** Aggressive imperial expansion in this era inevitably led to conflict and rebellion against the British. The Indian War of Independence and the Boer War in South Africa would epitomise this.

- **Religion:** Christian missionaries felt they had a moral duty to spread the message of Christianity throughout the world, especially to those they felt were in a 'lesser state of development'.

- **Government:** Parliament became more directly involved in the governing of empire, wanting to keep tighter control over British interests.

- **Ideas:** Social Darwinism and other ideas around white superiority emerged during this period and were used as justification for the idea of European racial domination of non-white people.

- **Science and technology:** Britain's navy was a vital part of developing the empire in this period. Furthermore, the development of railways built in Britain and throughout the empire helped to improve trade and communication.

- **Economic resources:** Britain began to industrialise and experience vast economic growth. Many new inventions helped to mechanise areas such as textiles and increase productivity and output. This in turn increased demand for raw products from the colonies, e.g. cotton.

- **Individuals:** Men such as Robert Clive and Cecil Rhodes would spearhead British expansion into new territories such as India and South Africa.

Britain wanted to gain control in India because of its economic resources and to stop other countries becoming powerful

- India was rich in natural resources such as iron, silk, copper, gold, silver, gemstones, tea and spices. Therefore, any country that was able to make trade links with India could become wealthy and powerful.

- Portugal discovered a sea route to India and established trading posts in the fifteenth century, which led it to become the first European power to dominate trade with India. It was replaced by the British and the Dutch in the sixteenth century and then the British and the French in the seventeenth century.

- India was ruled by local princes who did not always get along. Indian states were fighting for control and often used European powers as allies. The Mughal rulers had lost their power by 1740 due to civil disputes, which made it easier for the Europeans to fill the power vacuum.

- European powers could demand rewards from Hindu princes they helped in these disputes. These rewards could goods or land. If the princes did not comply, the Europeans would take what they wanted by force.

British trade in India was run by the East India Company (EIC)

- The East India Company was set up in 1600. Elizabeth I granted it the monopoly on English trade with south and east Asia, including India.

- The company carried British goods abroad for exchange, with goods from countries as far away as China and Japan. Its ships brought back goods such as china, silk, coffee and spices. The merchants in charge of the company and the kings and queens to whom they paid taxes became very wealthy.

- Between 1740 and 1767 the EIC wanted to expand its influence in India to maintain its economic interests, so began building a private army of its own.

- Nabobs were EIC officials who were able to act as middlemen in trade and other disputes between Indian princes. They became extremely wealthy and influential. Most EIC workers received low pay and worked in poor conditions.

Robert Clive and Warren Hastings played a major role in expanding the EIC's role and territory in India

Robert Clive	Warren Hastings
• Robert Clive was an officer in the East India Company's armed forces. • At the Battle of Arcot in 1751, he defeated the French and their Indian allies. • At the Battle of Plassey in 1757, he defeated the Nawab of Bengal. • Clive secured the state of Bengal as a power base for the British. • In 1765 he secured the Treaty of Allahabad. The British were now governing in India as they were now collecting tax revenues. • He became very wealthy. In 1753 he returned to Britain with enough money to pay to be selected for Parliament. • Clive died suspiciously in 1774 – many believe it was due to an ongoing opium addiction.	• Served with Clive during the Battle of Plassey. • In 1757, he resigned from the EIC as he didn't like the harsh treatment of the Bengalis. He resumed service with the EIC in 1769 and became governor-general of Bengal and British India in 1773. • Hastings valued Indian culture, promoting the learning of Indian language and literature. He encouraged the British and Indians to mix socially. • Hastings also supported British expansion and the use of the army in India. • Hastings became one of the wealthiest men in Britain and was put on trial for corruption and mismanagement of EIC funds in 1784. • The British government decided that the EIC could not be trusted to rule India alone. The 1784 India Act gave Parliament in Westminster joint control of India alongside the EIC.

 Test yourself

1 Give two reasons why the British became increasingly interested in India.

2 What does EIC stand for and when was it set up?

 Eliminate irrelevance

Explain the significance of Warren Hastings in bringing about changes to British rule in India.　　(8 marks)

It's important in a timed exam that everything you write is relevant. The paragraph below is from an answer to Question 3 above. Cross out anything irrelevant which does not help answer this question.

> Hastings is often credited for laying the foundation for the British rule in India along with Robert Clive. After becoming general of Bengal in 1773, Hastings orchestrated the building of a Muslim school in Calcutta. As someone who valued Indian culture, Hastings saw the benefits in promoting Indian language and literature, believing that this would strengthen ties between the British and Indians. Warren Hastings amassed a personal fortune of £220,000 by 1784, making him one of the wealthiest men in Britain. Hastings was interested in developing British power and was an advocate of using the army as a means of controlling more Indian territories during his stint as governor.

 Key individuals

Complete contact cards for Robert Clive and Warren Hastings. (see page 27).

 Practice question

Explain the significance of Robert Clive to the development of British control in India.　　(8 marks)

TIP

When considering the significance of an individual rather than an event, make sure you still consider the factors in your assessment. You could use your factors card on Robert Clive to help you answer this question.

3.2 The Great Rebellion, 1857

Direct British rule in India had a great impact on both Britain and India: socially, politically, culturally and economically

- The British viewed themselves as culturally superior to the Indians. In the 1830s and 1840s, they began making moves to take more direct control over Indian territory.
- The Doctrine of Lapse was introduced, banning Indian princes without a natural successor from choosing an heir. When they died, their land would now be under British control.
- An increased number of Christian missionaries began spreading Christian teachings. This angered many Indians, who felt that traditional religious practices were being replaced.
- The British also began to meddle in religious and cultural customs, such as allowing Hindu widows to remarry, which angered many.
- They also banned the Hindu tradition of suttee, when a widow would throw herself on top of the funeral pyre of her dead husband.

> **Key point**
>
> The Great Rebellion of 1857 would change the way the British Empire was governed, with the East India Company being replaced. The Rebellion would also stimulate the debate for Indian independence.

The Great Rebellion of 1857 was a revolt against British officers in the armies of the East India Company, triggered by unfair treatment of native Indian troops

- Most soldiers within the EIC's private armies were native Indian troops (Sepoys). The majority of Sepoys were Hindu, with roughly a quarter being Muslim. All officers were British.
- Many of the Sepoys felt they were being treated unfairly. They had little scope for promotion and were often sent on dangerous expeditions.
- Anger heightened in 1857 when new rifles were delivered. The cartridges that fired the rifles had to be bitten but they were greased in a mixture of pig and cow fat. Cows are sacred to Hindus and Muslims are forbidden from eating pork. The British refused to listen to the many protests.
- On 9 May 1857 in Meerut, 85 Sepoys refused to use the cartridges. They were arrested and sentenced to prison for 10 years. The day after, a group of Sepoys started a revolt, killing British people, freeing the imprisoned Sepoys and setting fire to the army barracks. Soon the rebellion had spread through northern India.
- The British sent 70,000 troops to supress the rebellion. Some captured Muslim mutineers were sewn into pig skins before being hanged. Others were strapped to the front of cannons which were then fired, blowing them apart. The Great Rebellion officially came to an end on 8 July 1858.

After the Great Rebellion the East India Company was abolished and Queen Victoria claimed that Indians were promised better treatment

- The British government was taken aback at the level of animosity that had been shown towards the British during the Great Rebellion. They decided to replace East India Company control with direct and total rule from the British Crown through the Government of India Act 1858. Indians were to be treated as 'equal subjects' within the British Empire.

There were some changes that the British deemed to be improvements:

○ The British tried to interfere less in education and religion.

○ Indians were offered more say in the running of India and jobs in government.

○ An Indian middle class started to emerge with the new opportunities. However, this was limited and driven by the caste system.

○ The Indian Universities Act created universities in Calcutta, Bombay and Madras.

● The queen and Parliament would nominate a secretary of state for India as well as a representative of the Queen, the viceroy. This new system was called the Raj. It lasted until Indian independence in 1947.

● Despite many of the new measures implemented in the Raj, Indians were still treated as inferior to the British.

● Trade to India would also begin to expand with the British acquisition of the **Suez Canal** in 1875 (see page 38).

● The Great Rebellion was a spark for nationalist movements to develop in India such as the Indian national Congress, created in 1885 and individuals such as Gandhi (see page 36).

 Test yourself

1 List reasons for the Sepoys being unhappy with how they were being treated.

2 How many British soldiers were sent to supress the Great Rebellion?

3 What system replaced the East India Company in India?

 Develop the detail

Complete the diagram below, adding detail to the areas where there were changes to how Britain ruled India after the Great Rebellion.

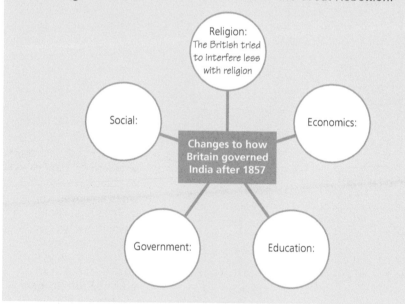

Religion: The British tried to interfere less with religion

Social:

Economics:

Changes to how Britain governed India after 1857

Government:

Education:

 Practice question

Explain the significance of the 1857 Indian rebellion to the development of the British Empire. (8 marks)

TIP

Always pay attention to the key words in the question. The question here asks about how the Indian rebellion led to further developments of the British Empire, not about the causes or events of the Indian rebellion itself. Make sure you cover at least two key developments, considering both short-term and long-term impacts.

 Consider significance

Because significance can seem quite a vague idea, it is easy to get sucked into including irrelevant details. All you really have to do with a significance question is explain one way the factor was significant at the time and one way it has been significant for people looking back from a later period.

Complete a table, giving points for how the Great Rebellion was significant at the time and how it was significant in later periods. You could use your completed spider diagram from 'Develop the detail' to help you.

3.3 Expansion in Africa

In the early nineteenth century, European interest and activity in Africa increased for a range of reasons

Key point

Between the late 1870s and 1900, European control of Africa rose from about 10 per cent to nearly 90 per cent. Britain acquired 16 areas of land, claiming 32 per cent of colonies in Africa by 1900.

Competition between European nations:
- European countries enjoyed the prestige of having colonies abroad and the power and wealth that colonies brought them.
- This led to competition between the most powerful nations in Europe to acquire foreign territories.

Christianity:
- British Christians wanted to spread the teachings of the Bible and convert African people to Christianity.
- Missionaries also wanted to improve people's lives and make sure that slavery was eradicated from African territories.

Why was there European interest in Africa and how did Britain become more involved in the early nineteenth century?

Commerce:
- After the slave trade was abolished, British traders wanted a more acceptable replacement.
- The industrial revolution required imports of products such as palm oil, widely found in West Africa.
- Europeans returned to their home countries with tales of gold, diamonds and ivory in other parts of Africa.

Civilisation:
- Africa was often referred to as the 'Dark Continent' by Europeans. Scientific racist ideas meant that African people were seen as inferior beings and that Europeans had a duty to bring its more 'civilised' values.
- In Britain the message of how the British could 'civilise' Africa became a central part of **imperial propaganda**.

From the mid-nineteenth century, several European powers started to claim colonies in Africa, which became known as the Scramble for Africa

- In the 1870s several European nations started to claim land in Africa. France and Belgium began to colonise large parts of West Africa while the British and Germans were interested in territories to the east and south. Portugal, Italy and Spain also started to gain an interest. This became known as the 'Scramble for Africa' as the countries desperately wanted to reach and claim colonies before other countries did.

- To avoid a clash among European nations, the great powers met in Berlin in 1884 to discuss how to keep peace in Africa. During this conference, Africa was divided up among the great powers. No African representatives were invited to these meetings.

Egypt became very important to Britain because it allowed quicker access to India

- India was by far the most profitable and important part of the British Empire. Travelling to India by ship from England meant sailing around Africa, which took a long time and could be dangerous because of rough seas and pirates. Therefore, quite early on in its relationship with India, Britain wanted to improve access over land in East Africa, including Egypt.

Imperial propaganda

- Books, magazines, adverts and even music all helped to spread positive messages about the empire so British people would support it.
- School textbooks were filled with stories about 'great empire builders' like Cecil Rhodes.
- The development of film meant that people were able to watch films that depicted positive views of the empire, even clips from battles during the Boer War (1899–1902).
- Events like Queen Victoria's Golden Jubilee in 1897 brought large groups of people together, in celebration of the British Empire.

- The Suez Canal, a waterway linking the Mediterranean to India, opened in 1869 under French control. In 1875, the British prime minister raised funds and bought a large number of shares in the canal from the Egyptian ruler Isma'il Pasha. The canal meant that goods could travel the entire way to India and back by ship without needing to sail around the whole of Africa.
- Egypt was never a formal colony of the British Empire but from this point on, Britain exerted considerable power there through investment and trade.

Test yourself

1 What is meant by the term 'Scramble for Africa'?

2 Why did Egypt become so important to Britain in the nineteenth century?

Develop the detail

Add details in the right-hand side of the table of how the factors in the left-hand side impacted on British interest in Africa. Try to use key terms from the information in this section.

Factor	Detail
Religion	
Government	
Ideas	

Spot the mistakes

This paragraph is about European expansion in Africa. It contains five factual errors. Cross out any information that is wrong and correct it.

European interest and involvement in Africa were stimulated by Competition, Commerce, Christianity and Civilisation. European competition for colonies led to the Berlin Conference in 1984, where the European powers came together to agree on how Africa ought to be divided. The Industrial Revolution required items such as palm oil, widely found in northern Africa. Africa was often referred to as the 'Light Continent' by Europeans who saw it as their duty to bring values such as democracy to the continent. Christian missionaries wanted to spread the teachings of the Bible throughout Africa in a bid to keep the slave trade going. A large number of Suez Canal shares were acquired by the British prime minister in 1876 as a way of improving sailing time to India.

Practice question

Explain two ways in which nineteenth-century British expansion in Africa and British expansion in America in the late sixteenth and the seventeenth centuries were similar.

(8 marks)

TIP

Consider the motives for these expansions and why they were different. For example, the factor of religion may have played a part in both eras of expansion, but the underlying reason may have been different.

3.4 British involvement in South Africa and the Boer War

> **Key point**
>
> The Boer War highlighted aggressive British expansion in Africa. Utilising nearly a quarter of a million soldiers, this conflict highlighted British military fragility and social issues back home in Britain.

The British competed with the Boers, descendants of Dutch migrants, for control in South Africa

- The Dutch had established a colony at the southern tip of Africa. In 1814 the British took control of this area that they called Cape Colony.
- The descendants of the Dutch migrants, known as the **Boers**, remained there, although many disliked British rule. When the British abolished slavery in the empire in 1833, the Boer farmers, who had many enslaved people, decided to leave and travel east and inland to find other settlements. They established the independent states of Transvaal (South African Republic) and the Orange Free State in the 1850s.

Cecil Rhodes expanded British territory in southern Africa

- Cecil Rhodes was an imperialist, believing that Britain was superior to other nations and should influence as much of the world as possible. He also strongly believed in Social Darwinism.
- In 1871 he and his brother took up diamond mining in southern Africa and became wealthy. In 1888 he set up De Beers, a company which would go on to own most of the mines in South Africa. He managed to trick King Lobengula to give away his rights to Matabeleland, which became Rhodesia.
- Rhodes became prime minister of Cape Colony in 1890 where he restricted the rights of black African people.

The Boer War was caused by rising tensions between the British and the Boers after gold was discovered in the Boer states

- Gold was discovered in the Boer states in 1886. Cecil Rhodes and other businessmen opened mines, which led to mass migration of British workers into Boer territory, causing conflict with the farmers who lived there.

- Paul Kruger, the Boer president, refused to give the British miners political rights and taxed the companies.
- In 1895–96 in the Jameson Raid, Rhodes attempted to remove Kruger by force and replace him with a British ruler, but this plan failed.
- This failed plan embarrassed the British government, which replaced Rhodes as premier of Cape Colony.
- The British government started to send troops to South Africa along the Boer border, which eventually led to the Boers declaring war in 1899.

The Boers did surprisingly well against the British forces, which led to brutal tactics by the British which eventually won the Boer War

- The Boer army consisted mainly of farmers but they were highly skilled fighters. They used modern guns from Germany and guerrilla tactics to surprise the British.
- After a series of defeats, the British government sent approximately half a million troops to fight 50,000 Boers.
- Under the command of General Kitchener, the British undertook a scorched earth policy, burning down Boer farms, killing their animals and poisoning their water. They put 116,000 Boer civilians into concentration camps where 28,000 died of disease due to the horrible conditions.
- The war came to an end in 1902 when the Boers finally surrendered.

There were several consequences of the Boer War for the British

- Although the British won the war, the British army had been humiliated and suffered the loss of 6,000 soldiers in battle and a further 16,000 from disease.
- Many of the young men who tried to join the British army to fight in the Boer War were deemed unfit for duty due to ill health, making the government look bad. This was one of the reasons why the government introduced a number of liberal reforms in 1906.
- The poor treatment of the Boers who had died in the camps shone a bad light on the British, with many questioning the empire.

Cecil Rhodes, 1853–1902

- Cecil Rhodes became one of the wealthiest men in Britain through his investment in the diamond business in southern Africa.
- He studied for his degree at Oriel College Oxford from 1883. There his belief in Social Darwinism developed.
- He took over the territory which would become Rhodesia and became prime minister of Cape Colony before trying to get more control of Boer states, which led to the Boer War, 1899–1902.
- Rhodes died in 1902, months before the Boer War ended.

Test yourself

1 What natural resources attracted British migrants to South Africa?
2 Describe what advantages the Boers had in combat.
3 List two ways in which the Boer War changed attitudes in Britain.

Consider usefulness

How useful is Source A to an historian studying British involvement in Africa in the nineteenth century?

(8 marks)

SOURCE A A cartoon about the British involvement in Africa published in an American weekly magazine, on 30 May 1900. The cartoon had the title, 'When the War is over'

Make notes in a grid like below to plan your answer.

Provenance	Content
Who made it and why?	What does it say about attitudes of the British in Africa?
	From your knowledge of events, is this accurate?
How does this affect its usefulness?	How does this affect its usefulness?

Key individuals

Complete a contact card for Cecil Rhodes (see top of this page).

Practice question

Explain the significance of Cecil Rhodes to the development of the British Empire in Africa.

(8 marks)

TIP

You may consider contemporary arguments in this answer. Rhodes remains a controversial figure, subject of many debates around ideas such as statues, both in Britain and in South Africa.

3.5 Migration to, from and within Britain in the nineteenth century

Key point

The mid to late nineteenth century saw many people on the move again, to, from and within Britain and the British Empire.

Motives	Experiences	Impact on Britain and empire
Irish migration to Britain		
From the late eighteenth century many Irish navvies migrated to big cities to find work. The 'potato blight' of 1846 meant many Irish were starving. Over half a million left their homes. By 1861, there were approximately 600,000 Irish-born people in Britain – mostly in Glasgow, Liverpool and London.	Catholic Irish migrants could face violence and persecution. The Irish could face difficulty finding work or suitable living conditions. They were blamed for crime and other social problems.	Irish migrants continued to arrive in Britain. The navvies built many of the British roads and railways. Many British soldiers during the First World War were Irish. The Easter Uprising of 1916 would be an important step towards Irish independence. To this day, Irish culture, e.g. music, plays a large part in societies across Britain.
Jewish migration to Britain		
Jewish people had been blamed for the assassination of the Russian Tsar Alexander II in 1881. In 1882, new laws persecuted Jewish people, placing them in poor areas, restricting their education and even expelling them altogether from places like Moscow (1891). Religious attacks on Jewish people called **pogroms** became commonplace as well.	The Jewish migrants were often charged high rents for poor conditions. Many Jewish people faced hostility as they were accused of stealing jobs. The British government passed the Alien Act to restrict immigration in 1905.	Jewish migrants retained their religious practices and opened the Jewish Free School in East London in 1822. Jewish migrants took up trades such as making clothes, shoes and furniture, becoming successful in these areas. Jewish people gained a reputation for being law-abiding citizens. Jewish communities remain important across British society with particularly large communities in places like London, Manchester and Glasgow.
Indian migration to Africa		
A large labour force was needed for the construction of the railways in Africa. Indian workers had constructed railways in India for the last 50 years. Nearly 30,000 Indian workers moved to the British African colonies of Kenya and Uganda to find work on the railways.	The pay and conditions for the workers were poor, with many succumbing to disease. In 1898 a pair of man-eating lions repeatedly attacked the railway workers, reportedly killing 28. The railway was dubbed the 'Lunatic Line' due to the danger of the project.	When the line was finished nearly 7,000 Indian workers remained in Africa. By the late 1960s there were around 180,000 'Kenyan Asians' and 60,000 'Ugandan Asians'. In the 1970s, there were expulsions against the Asian communities in Uganda, with many fleeing to Britain.
British migration to Australia		
In 1770, James Cook, a British navigator, landed in Australia. The British government decided to send convicts to Australia in a bid to empty the prisons. This was called **transportation** and is another example of forced migration.	The convicts started building settlements. Many decided to stay in Australia once their prison sentence was complete. The Aboriginal peoples (indigenous peoples) were forced off their land and many were killed.	Britain eventually claimed the whole of Australia as part of the British Empire. Australian soldiers would fight for Britain during the First World War. To this day, Australia is closely tied to Britain through the Commonwealth and many Brits still choose to migrate to Australia and vice versa.

Many migrants moved from rural to urban settings in Britain in the nineteenth century

- Britain's population in 1801 was 10 million; by 1901 it was 37 million.
- During the nineteenth century Britain was transformed, with many cities growing in population.
- In 1740, 80 per cent of people worked and lived in the countryside; by 1901, 75 per cent of people were living and working in larger towns and cities.
- Many sought work in cities and were able to migrate easily due to the new railways.
- This was mostly internal migration (within Britain), but job opportunities also attracted overseas migrants seeking work from places like Ireland.
- The larger towns grew, the more jobs were created, which in turn attracted more migrants.

> **TIP**
>
> Remember that 'migration' means 'people moving from one place to another'. Students often think this means people choosing to permanently live in another country but it also includes people moving to another part of the same country (internal migration), people being forced to move (forced migration) or people moving only for a short time before moving back again.

 Test yourself

1 Explain how Irish and Jewish immigrants were treated upon arrival in Britain.
2 Why were there Indians in Uganda in the nineteenth century?
3 Who 'discovered' Australia in 1770?

 The role of factors

Record examples of each of the following factors affecting migration to, from and within the British Empire during the nineteenth century. Give examples from the case studies above.

- War
- Religion
- Government
- Economic resources
- Science and technology
- Ideas

For each factor, outline how it affected migration.

 Change and continuity tables

Complete the factors table and change and continuity table for Part 3 Expansion and empire. See page 44.

 Practice question

Explain two ways in which Jewish migration to Britain in the nineteenth century and Huguenot migration to Britain in the seventeenth century were similar. (8 marks)

4.1 The end of empire

There were many factors in the twentieth century that influenced Britain's dealings with the world

- **War:** Many people migrated to Britain as a result of both world wars and regional wars.
- **Religion:** After the Second World War Britain became increasingly secular (non-religious); however, migration to Britain during the twentieth century led to a far more **multicultural** society with many differing religious beliefs.
- **Government:** The rise of the USSR and the USA made Britain reassess its international position. Joining the EU created a debate about who had control of sovereignty.
- **Ideas:** Nationalism drove liberation movements in colonies seeking independence.
- **Science and technology:** The development of air travel and other improved forms of transport made migration easier.
- **Economic resources:** Britain moved the focus of trade from empire to Europe.
- **Individuals:** Kwame Nkrumah led Gold Coast to independence, Jomo Kenyatta led Kenya to independence. Claudia Jones set up the Notting Hill Carnival.

The two world wars drained the economy and led to a loss of international power and prestige for Britain

- Before the First World War Britain was the world's leading power. After four years of fighting it was nearly bankrupt and had to borrow billions of dollars from the USA and Canada. This reduced Britain's international prestige.
- By 1914 the British colonies of Canada, Australia, New Zealand and South Africa had been granted **dominion status** (self-rule). This reduced the amount of central control from London. Dominion status was not given to countries where the population was not white, as those in Britain still strongly believed in Social Darwinism.
- The rise of **nationalism** drove the demand for independence in British colonies. Millions of colonial soldiers had contributed to both world wars and wanted to be rewarded with their own independent nation states.
- Trade was hugely disrupted by the international conflicts. This meant that colonies that relied on Britain for goods couldn't get them and built up their own industries, or the USA captured their markets. This reduced Britain's trading capacity.
- The Second World War bankrupted Britain. More people believed that the huge expense of maintaining the British Empire was not worth it, especially as the economy shifted to focus on trade with Europe and the USA.
- From 1945 Britain's international prestige was overshadowed by **Cold War** politics between the USA and the USSR. Britain was now in the top five of influential countries as opposed to being number one before 1914.
- During and after the Second World War there was a 'leftward swing' in British politics. Labour won the 1945 election. Rebuilding Britain through the welfare state was more important than the prestige of empire.
- Economically, the 'balance sheet' of empire was expensive – what Britain paid into it was less than what she got out of it. This led to **decolonisation**.

> **Key point**
>
> The First and Second World Wars were expensive and Britain lost lots of wealth and international prestige. Empire was expensive and Britain was looking for new trading partners.

> **Mohandas Gandhi, 1869–1948**
>
> - Mohandas Gandhi trained to become a lawyer in Britain, then went to work in South Africa in 1893. He started the **Indian National Congress** in 1885 to advance Indian rights in South Africa.
> - Gandhi returned to India in 1914 and became a leading campaigner for Indian independence using satyagraha – mass non-cooperation – leading huge non-violent protest, especially in 1920–22 and 1930–31.
> - He led the Indian National Congress with Jawaharlal Nehru in the 1940s, which pressurised the British into leaving India, which it did in 1947.
> - Gandhi was dismayed by partition and horrified by the violence that accompanied it. He tried to smooth things over but was murdered by a Hindu nationalist in January 1948.

Nationalism drove the demand for independence for India and other parts of the empire followed suit

- Across all British colonies there was a revival of pre-British cultural identity and a rise of nationalism from the start of the twentieth century.
- India, inspired by Gandhi's ideas of satyagraha, led demands for independence throughout the British Empire.
- Many Indian nationalists began demanding home rule after the First World War. Home Rule was similar to the dominion status of the White colonies.
- Indian protests led to the Amritsar Massacre of April 1919, which resulted in hundreds of Indians being killed by British soldiers. This led to increased demands for full independence.
- The British-style education system in India had created an informed middle class (people such as doctors and teachers), who spread political ideas and demanded freedom. This was similar in other parts of the empire, too.
- The Second World War increased demands for independence in India and elsewhere. Afro-Caribbean, African and Indian people had fought against **fascism** in Europe and Asia. They believed that they too should be free of an occupying force (Britain).
- Clement Atlee's Labour party agreed to Indian partition, a split between India and Pakistan, after the war. This led to independence for India in 1947 but resulted in widespread rioting and millions of deaths.

 ### Compare events

Question 3 will ask you to compare two key events from any part of the course. You will be asked to 'explain two ways' in which these events were either similar or different.

Make a list of similarities and differences between England's loss of European land in medieval times and the loss of the British Empire in the twentieth century.

- Causes
- Events
- Consequences

 ### Develop the detail

The diagram below gives factors that were important in decolonisation in the twentieth century. Add detail to explain each factor. Remember to include points on why Britain was willing to decolonise as well as why colonies wanted independence.

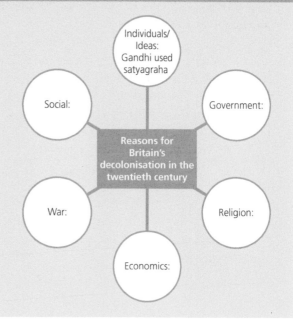

 ### Practice question

Explain two ways in which England's loss of European land in medieval times and the loss of the British Empire in the twentieth century were similar. [8 marks]

TIP

Remember to use as many key terms in your answers to exam questions as possible. Using specialist language, such as satyagraha, really demonstrates your knowledge.

 ### Test yourself

1 Explain the term satyagraha.
2 Give two reasons why there was more demand for independence from British colonies after the Second World War.
3 Why did Britain give dominion status to some but not all colonies?

4.2 The Suez Crisis and independence in Africa

The Suez Crisis lost Britain international prestige and it was a major turning point in Britain's relationship with its empire

- In 1956 Egypt's President Nasser nationalised the Suez Canal which had been owned by Britain and France. When talks collapsed, Britain, France and Israeli troops invaded Egypt. Much of the world, including the USA and the United Nations, condemned the action and troops were withdrawn. In Britain, Prime Minister Eden was forced to resign.
- The Suez Crisis caused great humiliation for Britain, resulting in a loss of international prestige. It was a major turning point in Britain's relationship with its colonies, especially those in Africa:
  - ○ Britain decided to grant independence to those nations that it felt were stable and would keep links with Britain. It wanted to stop the expansion of communism through developing a **commonwealth** of former empire nations to maintain close political and economic ties.
  - ○ Suez inspired other colonies that were not granted independence, such as Gold Coast and Kenya, to strive for it.

Kwame Nkrumah led a peaceful transition to independence in Gold Coast

- Many Ghanaians had fought in the West Africa Regiment in the Second World War and felt they deserved independence.
- Kwame Nkrumah did not want to wait for the British to slowly change the situation in Gold Coast. He was imprisoned for his views. However, he was very popular in Gold Coast and won the 1951 election while in jail. He was branded a communist by the British but they agreed to honour the election result and Nkrumah became leader of Gold Coast.
- Nkrumah was re-elected in 1956 and led a peaceful transition to independence in what became Ghana in 1957. He became the first black African leader of any former colony.

Kenya's struggle for independence was violent

- During the 1940s there were peaceful political demands for independence led by the Kenya African Union (KAU) whose leader was Jomo Kenyatta from 1947.
- At the same time, the Mau Mau anti-colonial resistance movement led a series of guerrilla attacks on Europeans and fellow African people who supported the British. The Mau Mau was known as the Land and Freedom Army because their land was being taken away by the British.
- East Africa had many white colonists, as there was excellent farmland and a good climate for Europeans. The Mau Mau wanted the land returned to African people and attacked the farms of many Europeans.
- The Mau Mau Rebellion led to an eight-year war. The British used torture and concentration camps to subdue Kenyans. This damaged Britain's moral authority.
- Kenyatta was branded and jailed (1953–61) as a communist and Mau Mau sympathiser by the British government (he wasn't).
- Hundreds died in the rebellion and as a result many white people migrated from Kenya.
- Independence was finally gained on 12 December 1963.

Key point

The **Suez Crisis** was a major turning point which exposed Britain's lack of international influence and further weakened its international prestige.

Kwame Nkrumah, 1909–72

- Kwame Nkrumah studied at universities in the USA and the UK but returned to Gold Coast in 1947 after being invited to work for the United Gold Coast Convention party.
- In 1949 he formed the Convention People's Party, which was more **radical** than the UGCC. He was put in prison by the British authorities but won the election in 1951.
- The British and Nkrumah decided to work together. Gold Coast became an independent country in 1957 with Nkrumah as its elected leader.

Jomo Kenyatta, c.1891–1978

- Jomo Kenyatta studied at universities in London before returning to Kenya in 1946.
- He was elected as leader of the Kenya Africa Union in 1947 and campaigned for independence.
- He was falsely accused of leading the Mau Mau uprising and imprisoned in 1961.
- Kenyatta became the first prime minister of independent Kenya in 1963 after leading the negotiations with the British government.

Test yourself

1 When was the Suez Crisis?
2 Give two reasons why some African colonies began to demand their independence from Britain.
3 What was the Mau Mau uprising?

 Key individuals

Complete contact cards for Mohandas Gandhi, Kwame Nkrumah and Jomo Kenyatta (see pages 36 and 38).

 Eliminate irrelevance

Explain the significance of the Suez Crisis to British rule in Africa. (8 marks)

It's important in a timed exam that everything you write is relevant. The paragraph below is from an answer to the question above. Cross out anything irrelevant which you think does not help answer this question.

Britain had gained many colonies in Africa in the nineteenth century including Kenya, Uganda, South Africa and Gold Coast. Although Egypt was not a British colony, the British had had great influence there because of its part ownership of the Suez Canal. When President Nasser of Egypt nationalised the canal in 1956, Britain, France and Israel sent troops to invade Egypt. This is known as the Suez Crisis. The invasion was condemned by most countries in the world and the United Nations, and the troops were withdrawn. The Suez Crisis was therefore significant as the British lost influence in Egypt. More than this, as Britain had already lost influence in the world after the Second World War, which economically devastated Britain, the Suez Crisis led to loss of international prestige as it was seen as a great humiliation for Britain.

 Practice question

Explain the significance of Mohandas Gandhi to the decolonisation of the British Empire. (8 marks)

TIP

For 'significance' questions, you need to identify **two** important points and explain them with evidence. 'Significance' means why someone or something was important. When it's asking about the significance of a person, think about their impact and discuss long- and short-term factors. Always use PEEL (Point – Explanation with Evidence – Link back to question).

4.2 The Suez Crisis and independence in Africa

4.3 The legacy of empire

There are many reasons why immigration to Britain from the Caribbean hugely increased in the 1950s

- On 22 June 1948, 492 Caribbean immigrants arrived at Tilbury Docks on the *Empire Windrush*. Although there had been migrants from the Caribbean in Britain before, these were the first of unprecedented numbers to arrive in Britain.

- The Caribbean had supplied more than 10,000 men to fight for Britain in the Second World War.

- These islands had been devastated by a hurricane in 1944 and poverty and hardship were commonplace. Migrants were looking for security and jobs.

- The actions of the British government encouraged migrants.

  ○ In 1948 Parliament passed the British Nationality Act – all people living in the empire (Commonwealth) were entitled to a British passport and allowed to live and work in Britain.

  ○ After the Second World War, Britain was short of workers, particularly in healthcare, transport and building, so advertised for migrants to come to Britain.

- Many in the Caribbean saw this as a great opportunity. They could apply for British passports and believed in 'king and country'. Many viewed Britain as the 'mother country'. Thousands decided to migrate to Britain.

Caribbean migrants had a difficult time in Britain, facing racism and even violence which activists such as Claudia Jones tried to combat

- The migrants met with prejudice and discrimination in most areas of life. Signs declaring 'No Black, No Dogs, No Irish' were common. There were even violent attacks on black men.

- Afro-Caribbean people were attacked by Teddy Boys in Nottingham and Notting Hill in 1958. These became known as Race Riots. This inspired Claudia Jones to set up the London Carnival (which later became the Notting Hill Carnival) to celebrate Caribbean culture and show the British some of what Caribbean people could contribute to Britain.

- The successful Bristol Bus Boycott of 1963 was led by black activist Paul Stephenson. His work inspired the Labour prime minister to introduce the first Race Relations Act in 1965, which made some racial discrimination illegal.

- However, continued oppression, alienation, police harassment and 'SUS' laws led to the Brixton Riots of April 1981.

- During the 1970s and 1980s right-wing extremists such as the National Front (NF) and British National Party (BNP) led anti-immigrant demonstrations into non-white areas of major cities.

- Incidents such as the New Cross house fire, which killed 13 young black people, and the Stephen Lawrence murder were not adequately investigated by the police.

- These were often countered by anti-racist groups like Rock Against Racism who organised gigs with bands such as The Clash, Steel Pulse and The Specials to raise awareness and fight back against racism.

- In Parliament BAME members such as Bernie Grant, Paul Boateng, Diane Abbott, Priti Patel and Rishi Sunak have made a great impact in politics.

Key point

Post-war migration to Britain brought a wealth of new ideas, culture, religion, food, language and identity to Britain but was often met with overt racism.

Claudia Jones (1915–64)

- Claudia Jones was from Trinidad but moved to New York. She became a political activist in the American civil rights movement. She was jailed in 1955 and deported to Britain.

- She led campaigns to combat racism and became a journalist. She established the *West Indian Gazette*.

- In response to the racist attacks of 1958, she started the London Carnival in 1959, held in St Pancras Hall. After her death in 1964, other activists worked together to make it into a street carnival and then it was known as the Notting Hill Carnival.

Key individuals

Complete contact cards for Claudia Jones and Idi Amin (see pages 40 and 41).

Major Idi Amin (1925–2003)

- Idi Amin fought in Kenya against the Mau Mau in 1952.

- He declared himself president and military leader of Uganda.

- In 1972 he declared 'economic war' against all Asian and European people in Uganda, taking over businesses and expelling all Asian people who were not Ugandan citizens.

Many Asian migrants also came to Britain from Uganda, Africa in the 1960 and 1970s

- Many Asian people in Africa decided to come to Britain in the 1960s as some newly independent African countries, including Uganda, increased discrimination against them.
- In 1968, the Conservative MP Enoch Powell gave his inflammatory 'Rivers of Blood' speech warning that more Caribbean and Asian immigration would lead to violence and called for the repatriation of migrants.
- The Labour government then introduced laws which restricted further migrants from coming to Britain.
- In 1972 President Idi Amin announced that Asian Ugandans that were not citizens would be expelled within 90 days. The Conservative government agreed to accept 29,000 to Britain.

The Falklands War was a successful attempt by Britain to defend one of its remaining colonies

- The Falkland Islands is part of the Commonwealth and was settled by British people in 1833. In 1982 it had a population of around 2,000 people.
- In 1982, Argentina was led by General Galtieri, a military dictator. He hoped to distract Argentines from severe economic problems by winning control of the nearby Falkland Islands. On 2 April, an Argentine force of 12,000 took control of the island.
- British prime minister Margaret Thatcher responded quickly and defiantly by sending over 100 ships and 28,000 troops. The Argentines surrendered on 14 June.
- Despite the huge cost of the Falklands War, it was a major boost to Thatcher and the jingoism that the war encouraged helped her to win the 1983 election.

Test yourself

1 Explain why there was migration to Britain after the Second World War.

2 Give an example of the impact that Claudia Jones had on British culture.

3 Give two examples of the impact of immigration on Britain from 1948.

TIP

For 'how useful' questions **three** is the magic number – in each paragraph you should write three points explained with evidence. Try to blend your own knowledge with your source analysis. Remember to use both what is in the source and the provenance above the source in your answer.

Practice question

How useful is Source A to an historian studying Caribbean migration to Britain in the twentieth century? Explain your answer using Source A and your contextual knowledge. (8 marks)

SOURCE A A cartoon, called 'Both sides of the Picture', published in 1954, from the British magazine Punch. Punch was a popular magazine which often used humour to comment on life in Britain and abroad at the time. It also sold many copies in British colonies. In 1953, Punch appointed a new editor who employed cartoonists with a harsher, more critical view of British life.

4.4 Britain's relationship with Europe and its impact

Most European countries have come closer together in greater union since the Second World War but Britain's relationship with Europe has oscillated

- To stop future conflict in Europe after the Second World War, the European Coal and Steel Community (ECSC) was set up in 1951. This developed into the European Economic Community (EEC) in 1957. Britain initially refused to join.

- Trade with Europe was easier and cheaper than with the Empire. As the EEC became very successful, Britain tried to join twice in the 1960s but was rejected.

- Under Edward Heath's Conservative government, Britain was finally accepted into the EEC in 1973. Denmark and Ireland joined at the same time.

- The Labour Party was unsure about Britain's membership so once in government from 1974 it held a **referendum** in 1975. Two-thirds of people voted to stay in the EEC.

- Margaret Thatcher supported the creation of the single market in 1980 – goods, services and people could move freely between all 12 EEC countries. It became the largest trading organisation in the world.

- John Major's Conservative government signed the Maastricht treaty in February 1992. This created the **European Union**, which transferred some power from the British Parliament to the European Parliament. Brexiteers regard this as a loss of national sovereignty and identity.

- In 1999, 12 members of the EU adopted the euro as a single currency but Tony Blair's Labour government decided to maintain the pound sterling.

The end of the Cold War brought many changes to Europe which affected Britain and the rest of the European Union

- The Cold War ended in the early 1990s and the USSR no longer had control over the countries of Eastern Europe. Many of these former communist countries wanted to join the EU for trade and remove themselves from Russian influence.

- In 2004 eight former communist Eastern European countries joined the EU. In 2007 Romania and Bulgaria joined, followed by Croatia in 2013. There were then 28 members of the European Union.

- This hugely affected migration as many Eastern Europeans migrated to other parts of the EU, mostly for economic reasons. Many came to Britain to work in the NHS, in construction, fruit picking and retail sectors. Some came for short-term work while others settled with their families. The largest group were from Poland.

- In 2015 there were 1.9 million migrants working in Britain – 60 per cent of those were from Eastern Europe.

- This had a significant cultural and social impact that benefited Britain, with, for example, new ideas, fashions, languages and food.

> **Key point**
>
> Joining the EEC which became the EU was contentious. It led to the free movement of goods and people, which had a major impact on British politics, economics and social change.

- Some, however, believed that this immigration damaged communities and put pressure on public services in some areas.
- At the same time, over 2 million Britons have migrated to other countries in the EU. More than 50 per cent of those migrants went to Spain.
- The 2008 Great Recession damaged hopes for greater EU integration in Britain.
- The 2016 referendum resulted in a narrow victory for the Leave campaign. The UK left the EU on 31 January 2020.

 ## The role of factors

Record examples of each of the following factors affecting migration to, from and within Britain during the twentieth century. Give examples from the case studies above.

- War
- Religion
- Government
- Economic resources
- Science and technology
- Ideas
- Individuals

For each factor, outline how it affected migration.

 ## Change and continuity tables

Complete the factors table and change and continuity table for Part 4 Britain in the twentieth century. See page 44.

 ## Exam technique

The final question in the exam will be an essay question where you have to evaluate a given factor against other factors. You must **make a judgement** to gain good marks. Aim to write four paragraphs:

1 STATED factor
2 Other factor
3 Other factor
4 Conclusion

Here is a list of words and phrases that can help you:

Firstly... Secondly... because/as... Consequently... Hence... Therefore... Since... Thus... So... Equally... Similarly... In the same way... As with... Likewise...

Counterargument

Nevertheless... Despite this... Alternatively... On the other hand... Whereas... However... Although...

Strengthening

In particular... Notably... more important... significantly... especially... Above all... For example... Such as... also... as well as... This suggests... clearly... of course... Naturally... Obviously... Evidently... Surely... Certainly... Furthermore... Moreover... in addition...

Conclusion

In conclusion... To sum up... finally... on the whole... Overall...

 ## Test yourself

1 What year did Britain join the EEC?
2 When was the Single Market created in Europe?
3 How did the expansion of the EU from 2004 affect migration to Britain?

 ## Practice question

Has war and violence been the main factor in causing the settlement of people in Britain? Explain your answer with reference to war and violence and other factors.

Use a range of examples from across your study of Migration, empires and the people: c.790 to the present day.   (16 marks) (SPaG 4 marks)

4.5 Factors and change and continuity

Factors

There are seven factors that influenced empire and migration that you need to bear in mind for this course. They helped cause change and they helped maintain continuity. An explanation of these factors is in the first column of the table below.

Complete the relevant column of the table for each period when you reach the end of that period. Then compare all four periods at the end.

	Part 1 Conquered and conquerors	Part 2 Looking west	Part 3 Expansion and empire	Part 4 Britain in the twentieth century
Individuals and **Ideas** Individuals influenced migration and empire. These were not only kings, queens and politicians but ordinary people taking extraordinary decisions.				
Government The people governing the country have had a direct effect on creating empires and driving migration through their decisions and policies.				
Religion Religious ideas have often justified the creation of empires and led to migration, e.g. through persecution.				
Economic resources Seeking wealth and increasing trade have been central reasons for migration and the creation of empires.				
War War, military expansion and violence or the threat of it have helped create, maintain and lose empires.				
Science and technology/social change New discoveries (science) and new inventions (technology) usually encourage change, including social change.				

Change and continuity

It is important to consider what changed and what remained the same during each period. At the end of each period, complete the table below with three things that changed (Change) and three things that remained the same (Continuity) in that period. Use the IGREWS factors to help you.

In the final row, circle the number in each column, where 1 is little and 10 is a lot. Write your explanation below, providing evidence to support it.

Change		Continuity	
1		1	
2		2	
3		3	
1 2 3 4 5 6 7 8 9 10		1 2 3 4 5 6 7 8 9 10	

> **TIP**
>
> IGREWS is a mnemonic to help you to remember the different factors:
>
> I = Individuals and ideas
>
> G = Government
>
> R = Religion
>
> E = Economic resources
>
> W = War
>
> S = Science and technology/social change.

Model answers

Here are model answers for each question type on the Thematic Study.
The annotations highlight what makes each one a good answer.

Question 1: Usefulness of a source

**Study Source A. How useful is Source A to an historian studying
Viking invasions of Britain?**

**Explain your answer using Source A and your contextual knowledge.
(8 marks)**

SOURCE A *An English
illuminated manuscript,
c1130, depicts Viking ships
attacking Britain*

Source A is useful as it shows an army of heavily armed Viking
warriors in longships attacking Britain. England was an easy target
as it was a divided land – the heptarchy made up of seven different
kingdoms, which were often at war with each other. Culturally, Vikings
were very different from the English and initially invaded for plunder
and pillage. They were from Norway and Denmark and were heathens
– non-Christians. They seemed to fear no one, looked very fierce and
regarded death in war as glorious. The first Viking attack was at
Lindisfarne monastery in 792 and by 1016 King Cnut had been able
to establish a North Sea empire. Many of the English believed the
Viking invasions had been sent as a punishment from God.

The source is also useful because it shows that two hundred years
after their first arrival, the threat of a Viking attack is still in the
mindset. It is from an English illuminated manuscript; these were
created by highly skilled monks. This one was written during the
Norman period and is perhaps a warning from history to make sure
that England is well defended against future invasions. It shows the
ferocity of the Vikings as an unregulated merchant warrior class.
No doubt the author did not want his monastery to be raided,
valuable religious items stolen and the monks taken as slaves and
transported in longboats to be sold at slave markets such as Dublin.

8-mark questions require
two-paragraph answers

The student uses key
words in the question stem

They use the content to
explain longships used for
war

This shows excellent own
knowledge

This links back to the
question using own
knowledge

The student uses the
provenance of the source
to evaluate its usefulness

This shows that longships
were used for transportation
of economic resources

8-mark questions require
two-paragraph answers

Question 2: Explain significance

**Explain the significance of Alfred the Great for Anglo-Saxon
England. (8 marks)**

Alfred the Great was significant to Anglo-Saxon England because his actions
led to the overall unification of England, where the decades of anarchy in the
heptarchy that was England came to an end. To do this he instilled confidence
and security into the nation, with burhs built in the 880s for defence, a new
law code featuring schools to train priests, and the encouragement of nobles

The answer is directed to
the question

The student backs up their
judgement with evidence

The answer is extended
using well-explained
evidence

to study and fight. Alfred used the Anglo-Saxon Chronicle to motivate the country to be more unified and aimed to have a unified and powerful England that could stand together against Viking invasion.

Furthermore, Alfred also used religion to lead the liberation of England. He had visited Rome twice and had met the Pope, which earned him the title as the 'defender' of all Christian Anglo-Saxons, and his push for Christianity boosted the unification of the country because all the regions could relate to each other. He proved his allegiance to the Church and the country by ultimately converting the Danish King Guthrum to Christianity after England won the Battle of Edington in 878, a surprising feat as two-thirds of England was under the Danelaw. Moreover, the Danish empire seemed to be halted. Overall, King Alfred the Great was clearly significant to Anglo-Saxon England because he laid the foundation for the unification and liberation of England.

This is a good connective

This is good use of evidence, explained well

The student extends the point

The student makes a judgement and links back to the question – so they use PEEL

Question 3: Compare events

Explain two ways in which England's loss of European land in medieval times and the loss of the British Empire in the twentieth century were similar. (8 marks)

Loss of European land in medieval times is similar to loss of the British Empire in the twentieth century because they were both inspired by and created the foundations of national identity. For example, after the Hundred Years War that finished in 1453, even though Henry II gained more land from the French, during the reign of King John this land was won back by the French. Due to the fact that only a fraction of France was left under British control, it led to the birth of English identity as it meant that the nation was more independent. As well as this, England stopped using the French language, symbolising English strength and honour, proven after the success at the Battle of Agincourt. Although, by the end of the Hundred Years War England had lost all land in France, apart from Calais. Much of their subsequent defeat was due to the emergence of Joan of Arc, who was able to unite the French in the struggle against the English.

This is similar to the loss of the British Empire because, due to a rise of nationalism in the early 1900s, for example inspired by Egypt's independence of 1922 and the nationalisation of the Suez Canal, colonies and nations manipulated by the empire became empowered and hungry for independence. Due to the fact that white colonies such as Canada were allowed dominion status by Britain, 'unstable colonies' began to demand independence. Gandhi, for example, protested about British control and unfair taxation through the massive salt marches of the 1930s, as well as helping India gain independence in 1947. This was the rebirth of Indian identity. Such power later inspired nationalists such as Kenyatta and Nkrumah to fight for their country in release from British control, much like the birth of British identity after the Hundred Years War.

This is a strong opening which uses the key words in the question

A factor is identified – it relates to Ideas

A key turning point is identified with evidence and explanation

This is related back to a key point

The student uses excellent evidence

The answer has two paragraphs – this is required for 8-mark questions

The second paragraph uses key words from the question

A second factor is identified – again Ideas

This is excellent evidence – explained well

This is a sophisticated link to ideas discussed in the previous paragraph

Here is a very high-level connection between both time periods

Question 4: Factor-based essay

Have economic factors been the main cause of people migrating from and within Britain?

Explain your answer with reference to economic and other factors.

Use a range of examples from across your study of Migration, empires and the people: c790 to the present day. (16 marks + 4 SPaG marks)

Clearly economic factors are the main cause of people migrating from and within Britain. They are always a major driving force of migration, such as with the Vikings from the 790s. Educated monks and other skilled Britons were highly prized as slaves and were transported from England and sold in slave markets such as Dublin. They often ended up in Scandinavia and even as far as Persia. Forced migration was very profitable for the Vikings. Viking raiders caused many Britons to move inland away from coastal raids. This shows that the Viking raids caused a lot of migration across Britain. Furthermore, in the eighteenth century many people moved within Britain as it changed drastically as a result of the industrial revolution. This brought mass job opportunities and as a result a multitude of people across Britain moved from rural to urban areas like London and Manchester. People were looking for new opportunities to improve their lives as well as leaving the drudgery of everyday life behind, clearly an example of economic impact on society.

> The answer opens by directly addressing the factor given in the question

> Here the paragraph links to the issue in the question

On the other hand, it could be argued that religious factors are the main cause of people migrating from and within Britain, Puritans, Quakers and Catholics to America from Britain after conflict with the Protestant Church. The Pilgrim Fathers moving from Plymouth to New England is a prime example of a religious group who faced persecution at home and moved from Britain for a 'New Jerusalem' in the Americas. Furthermore, as a result of the Highland Clearances, many Catholic Scots were forced into urban centres like Glasgow and Dundee and to the USA, Australia and New Zealand by their Protestant landowners, which shows how strong religion's impact is on people migrating from and within Britain. Moreover, government is a force for people migrating from and within Britain. When England was controlled by the Danelaw pressured and angered Anglo-Saxons moved to Wessex to be under the Christian rule of Alfred the Great and not the pagan Vikings. Britons also moved as a result of Margaret Thatcher's support of the creation of the Single Market in 1980. This meant that goods, services and people could move freely between all 12 EEC countries. Over 2 million Britons moved to Europe. In conclusion, despite the other factors such as religion and government being highly relevant, the most important factor is economics. This is due to the fact that the desire for personal or national wealth was the main driving force from the Viking period to Brexit. During the imperial period, Britain aimed to be the greatest economic power and it could be argued that this was the driving force behind expansion. As such, they needed workers in newly conquered lands to help develop and bolster Britain's economy.

> There is good use of argumentative language to show counterargument and introduce other factors

> The answer extends the Religious factor and interlinks with economic reasons for movement and re A third factor is identified lates to 'from and within'

> A third factor is identified

> The student makes strong use of evidence to compare the first area of study and the fourth

> This interlinks government and economics and relates back to the question

Glossary

Anarchy   A state of disorder due to absence or non-recognition of authority or other controlling systems

Angevins   A royal house that ruled England in the twelfth and early thirteenth centuries; its monarchs were Henry II, Richard I and John

Anglo-Saxon Chronicle   Chronological account of events in Anglo-Saxon and Norman England, written by monks.

Boers   Descendants of the original Dutch settlers in South Africa – most are farmers

Burhs   Fortresses or castles that King Alfred set up across England in the 880s for defence

Christendom   The Church's sphere of power and authority, both politically and spiritually, in Europe during the Middle Ages

Christianity   By 800 AD most of Britain had converted to this religion

Cold War   A conflict between the USA and the Soviet Union. The nations never directly confronted each other on the battlefield but deadly threats went on for years

Colonialism   A policy by which a nation administers a foreign territory and develops its resources for the benefit of the colonial power

Colour bar   A social system which does not allow black people the same rights as white people

Commerce   The conduct of trade that was an important activity throughout the Middle Ages

Commodity   A raw material or primary agricultural product that can be bought and sold, such as copper or coffee

Commonwealth   A political system in which the supreme power lies in a body of citizens who can elect people to represent them

Danegeld   A tax raised to pay tribute to the Viking raiders to save a land from being ravaged. It was called the geld or gafol in eleventh-century sources

Danelaw   Historical name given to the part of England in which the laws of the Danes held sway and dominated those of the Anglo-Saxons

Decolonisation   The action or process of a state withdrawing from a former colony, leaving it independent

Dominion status   The status, prior to 1939, of each of the British Commonwealth countries of Canada, Australia, New Zealand, the Union of South Africa, Eire and Newfoundland

Dynastic politics   A family who belonged to power and wealth and wanted their members to inherit land and authority

Dynasty   A line of hereditary rulers of a country

Empire   An extensive group of states or countries under a single supreme authority, formerly especially an emperor or empress

European Union   An international organisation of European countries formed after the Second World War to reduce trade barriers and increase cooperation among its members

Fascism   A political system based on a very powerful leader, state control, and being extremely proud of country and race, and in which political opposition is not allowed

Heptarchy   A collective name applied to seven Anglo-Saxon kingdoms. Existed between the sixth and ninth centuries

Huguenots   French Protestants that escaped from religious persecution.

Imperial propaganda   Positive aspects, ideas and information about the empire were spread in order to influence public opinion and belief

Imperialism   A policy in which a strong nation seeks to dominate other countries politically, socially and economically, extending a country's power and influence through diplomacy or military force

Indentured servants   Would work until their contract was finished and then would get paid to work

Indian National Congress   A movement and political party founded in 1885 to demand greater Indian participation in government. Led after 1920 by Mohandas K. Gandhi

Magna Carta   King John was challenged by the barons and promised to respect the rights of the Church and the barons and stop unfair taxes

Mercantilism   Law under which only British ships were allowed to transport goods

Multiculturalism   The co-existence of diverse cultures

Nationalism   A strong feeling of pride in and devotion to one's country

Patrial   A person with the right to live in the UK through the British birth of a parent or grandparent

Plantation   A large area of farmland devoted to a single cash crop

Pogrom   Religious attack

Puritans   Strict Protestant Christians

Radical   Believing or expressing the belief that there should be great or extreme social or political change

Reformation   A religious movement of the sixteenth century that began as an attempt to reform the Roman Catholic Church and resulted in the creation of Protestant churches

Social Darwinism   A white supremacist idea to justify expansion and conquest. The application of ideas about evolution and 'survival of the fittest' to human societies – particularly as a justification for their imperialist expansion

Transportation   The forced migration of prisoners to America and Australia in the 1700s and 1800s